"Christians are ordinary people who worship and serve an extraordinary God! This God, revealed preeminently in Jesus Christ, has a special concern for the abused, the enslaved, the fatherless, the poor, the stranger, the widow. And, He has seen fit to care for these who bear His image through His people. *Ordinary* is a theologically rich, practical guide in how anyone can get involved in caring for those this broken world all too often abuses, exploits, and ignores. These precious people matter to our God. Therefore, they should matter to us. Tony Merida points the way in how to get going. Are you ready? Are you willing?"

Daniel L. Akin, president, Southeastern Baptist Theological Seminary, and editor of Christ-Centered Exposition Commentary

"Nothing is more radical than the ordinary lived in consistent, humble, unassuming, selfless faithfulness to God for the sake of His work and witness. Merida wonderfully explore what it could mean today for Christ's followers to live faithfully amidst life's ordinary challenges for a radical testimony of God's grace to family, neighbor, and watching world. This is what it means for others to see our ordinary deeds and give glory to our Father in heaven for the extraordinary mercy of His Son."

Bryan Chapell, pastor, Grace Presbyterian Church and author of *The Gospel According to Daniel*

"*Ordinary* is not an ordinary book! My friend Dr. Tony Merida takes you on a journey that will deepen and thicken your faith-connection to Jesus. You will see justice and compassion with new eyes and new affections that will compel you to join Jesus in turning the world upside down."

Derwin L. Gray, lead pastor, Transformation Church and author of *Limitless Life*

"Tony writes with simple causal clarity, radical God-centeredness, and contagious missional focus. This is Christianity at its simplest and purest. This book will not only wreck you emotionally, it will change your life—it's extraordinary."

J.D. Greear, pastor, The Summit Church and author of *Stop Asking Jesus Into Your Heart*

"It's God's habit to do extraordinary feats through ordinary people. Often believers sit on the sidelines of life paralyzed by fear assuming they're too ordinary for God to use. Tony Merida's encouraging words will do nothing less than jump-start the heart of the reader to live on mission for God. If you've been asking "How," God wants to use you and this book will shed light on God's prescribed answer in Scripture."

D. A. Horton, executive director of ReachLife Ministries

"This book puts it plainly—ordinary people doing simple acts of kindness, justice, and mercy can change the world. Rather than pontificate on what others should be doing, Tony challenges you to get busy doing what you can do, where you are, with what you have to impact others. Less talk, more action—that's the message!"

Jeff Iorg, president, Golden Gate Seminary and author of *Seasons of a Leader's Life*

"I especially admire how integrative this book is. Tony consistently shows that the gospel of grace is the basis for ministry of both word and deed, for evangelism and social action. He accentuates the harmony of the Old Testament and New Testament accounts of justice. He draws out how worship, prayer, Scripture, community, and hospitality all work together in the life of a committed Christian. He motivates through the dynamics of the gospel, rather than through emotional appeals. And in doing all this, he is completely practical without being pragmatic."

Timothy Keller, pastor, Redeemer Presbyterian Church and author of *The Reason for God* and *Generous Justice*

"Tony wrote a must-read and fresh perspective on justice, mercy, and serving the poor. He is an academic, pastor, and practitioner, and he brings vulnerability and passion through his words. This book promotes a holistic framework on seeking justice and serving the poor as an 'ordinary' part of Christian living. Read it and live it."

Chris Marlow, founder and CEO of Help One Now

"When I think of the name Tony Merida, I immediately think of anointing. The Spirit of God is present all over his ministry, and not just in the pulpit, but in the way that he lives his life. This book on turning the world upside down is part of the result of that dynamic anointing. You will be challenged by this book and called to consider the claims of Christ in areas of life you may never have considered before. This book equips us with wisdom and prepares us for action."

Russell D. Moore, president, Southern Baptist Ethics & Religious Liberty Commission and author of *Tempted and Tried*

"*Ordinary* by Tony Merida is exactly the kind of book you want to read if you feel the brokenness of the world around you and are looking for biblical, practical ways to engage that brokenness. If we had more ordinary Christians in the way Tony Merida describes them there would be more meaningful impact in this world by Christians in the church. This book broke me, stirred me, and also gave me tools to move forward with action."

Harvey Turner, founding and preaching pastor, Living Stones Churches and network director for Acts 29 West

ORDINARY

~~EXTRA~~ ORDINARY

HOW TO ~~CONQUER~~ turn
THE WORLD upside down

TONY MERIDA

B&H
PUBLISHING GROUP
Nashville, Tennessee

978-1-4336-8416-6

Published by B&H Publishing Group
Nashville, Tennessee

Dewey Decimal Classification: 259
Subject Heading: MINISTRY \ HELPING BEHAVIOR \
CHRISTIAN LIFE

1 2 3 4 5 6 7 8 19 18 17 16 15

For the voiceless, powerless, and vulnerable;
for the least of these.

Acknowledgments

First of all, I am indebted most of all to Jesus Christ. Thank You for justifying the ungodly, like me. I long for Your return, when You make all sad things untrue; where we enjoy the eternal comfort of living in a perfectly just world.

Second, I owe more than I can give to my wife and family. Kimberly, you are my "justice girl," and sweet companion in the cause; "The heart of her husband trusts in her" (Prov. 31:11). To my five kids, James Arthur, Angela Grace, Jana Sophia, Victoria Joy, and Joshua Livingstone: may God raise you up and make you gospel-loving, justice-pursuing servants of Jesus. My parents, Gary and Brenda, have modeled generosity and simplicity to me for years; thank you.

Imago Dei Church family, may God use us to preach grace and do justice to the ends of the earth.

I am indebted to four men, three of whom are personal friends, for sharpening me on issues in this book: Tim Keller, Russell Moore, Steve Timmis, and David Platt. Keller has helped me think through issues related to gospel and justice. Moore has helped me better understand the Kingdom. Timmis gave us the phrase, "ordinary people doing ordinary things with gospel intentionality," and has really elevated my view of hospitality. Platt has encouraged me for years, particularly with his emphasis on global missions. I hope to echo much of *Radical* in *Ordinary*, with some of my own applications.

When Devin Maddox asked me to write this book, my reaction was negative. But I'm glad he made me do it! This has been a very sanctifying process, and I pray that the material here will help many believers and churches. So, thank you, Devin, for messing up my life! For real, I'm grateful to you and the B&H team for printing *Ordinary*. It's a blessing to work with a publishing team that believes in the message and mission of this book, and views their work as ministry, not merely as a business.

Contents

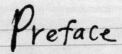

Preface

> "These men . . . have turned the world upside down . . . saying that there is another king—Jesus!"
>
> Acts 17:6–7 HCSB

How were these early Christians turning the world upside down? They had a different King, Jesus, who called them to a unique way of life. They weren't impressive people, but they had an impressive King.

The book of Acts shows that the result of the early church's efforts wasn't due to their own gifting and wealth (though some were gifted and wealthy). When Peter and John were brought before the council they were called "unschooled, *ordinary men*" (Acts 4:13 NIV, my emphasis). Not even the leaders were extraordinary!

But these ordinary people turned the world upside down.

By submitting to the lordship of Jesus, proclaiming His substitutionary death and bodily resurrection, and displaying good deeds that reflect the values of the Kingdom, God used these ordinary Christians to change lives—one conversation at a time, one meal at a time, one act of mercy at a time.

When Paul and his missionary team went to Philippi, they started the first church on European soil. That sounds amazing, but it actually started in a very humble way. There were no light shows. The mission team went down by a river, where some ordinary women were gathered together. It looked like nothing more than a picnic with some prayers. I bet many people walked right past these ladies. But as the team approached them, and as Paul taught the gospel, God worked in the heart of a lady named Lydia to understand and believe the gospel. (That is an extraordinary thing!) Afterward, some others believed in the city, and the church got established. It more than likely met in Lydia's home initially—not a majestic sanctuary, but a home. God opened her heart, and she opened her home. Ordinary people, redeemed by the King, then set out to live on mission, like we are called to do.

A few years after the book of Acts, a man named Aristides commented on the reasons for the influence of Christianity. He wrote to Emperor Hadrian in AD 125, noting some very "nonsensational," but truly beautiful acts of mercy. Here is what he said described these Christians:

> Further, if one or other of them have bondmen and
> bondwomen or children, through love towards them they
> persuade them to become Christians, and when they have
> done so, they call them *brethren* without distinction. They
> do not worship strange gods, and they go their way in all
> *modesty and cheerfulness. Falsehood is not found* among them;
> and they *love one another*, and from *widows* they do not
> turn away their esteem; and they deliver *the orphan* from
> him who treats him harshly. And *he, who has, gives to him*
> who has not, *without boasting.* And when they *see a stranger,*
> *they take him in to their homes and rejoice over him as a very*
> *brother*; for they do not call them brethren after the flesh,
> but brethren after the spirit and in God. And whenever
> one of their poor passes from the world, *each one of them*
> *according to his ability gives heed* to him and carefully sees
> to his burial. And if they hear that one of their number is

imprisoned or afflicted on account of the name of their Messiah, all of them anxiously minister to his necessity, and if it is possible to redeem him they set him free. And if there is among them any that is *poor and needy*, and if they have no spare food, *they fast* two or three days in order to supply to the needy their lack of food.[1]

In other words, they lived as though there was another King.

In the following pages, I want to reflect on some of these types of acts described by Aristides. My prayer is that we would see a recovery of such movement, an "ordinary movement," that involves ordinary Christians, not just the "super Christians," who live on mission in the rhythms of everyday life. Ordinary Christians who proclaim an extraordinary message, and ordinary Christians who practice compelling acts of justice and mercy.

And I pray that we can see this movement happening not just with individual Christians, but with churches. We are called to live out our Christian life in community. The church is God's primary mission strategy that seeks to live out the values of the King. The church is an outpost of the Kingdom. About ten years after Paul started the church in Philippi, he wrote a letter to them. He said their "citizenship [was] in heaven" (Phil. 3:20). Realize that no ancient city was more like Rome than Philippi. When you visited Philippi, you would say, "This reminds me of Rome." That sort of thing happens today when you visit a U.S. Embassy in another country. Yet, Paul calls the church "citizens of heaven." In other words, the church was a little embassy of the Kingdom; the church was an outpost of the Kingdom. When people look at your local church they should say, "This way of life reminds me of the Kingdom to come."

That will happen only when we reject the prevailing philosophies of our day, and instead live as though there really is another King, Jesus, who reigns and is coming soon to establish His glorious Kingdom.

Introduction
Confessions

Trading Sensationalism for Ordinary Christianity

"I put on righteousness, and it clothed me;
my justice was like a robe and a turban."

JOB 29:14

"Will you lead a Bible study focusing on *the poor* each morning?"

No problem, I thought. *I'll just survey the Bible, pull some passages together, tell a few stories, and it will be a fruitful week of student camp.*

I don't recall a ton of students testifying about the impact of this particular study, but one thing definitely happened: it wrecked *me*. Soon my wife and I would reorient our lives, adopt five children, begin fighting human trafficking, and seek to put into practice what you're about to read in this book.

Ministries of mercy and justice weren't very important to me until about six years ago. I became a follower of Christ in college. I soon surrendered to ministry, and went to New Orleans for seminary. I finished three degrees, pastored a church in New Orleans, and then went on faculty at the same seminary where I had been a student. While my wife had been doing inner-city ministry in New Orleans, I occasionally ministered to the poor. I never considered mercy and justice ministry central to my life. I was a preacher. A pastor. A professor.

Then I taught this Bible study.

As I began to survey the Scriptures, and considered the wisdom of other evangelical writers, I began to see afresh God's concern for the poor. I was struck by texts on God's mercy and justice. The psalmists write: "The King in his might *loves justice*"[2] and "The LORD works righteousness and justice for all who are oppressed."[3] I began to see the repeated emphasis on the *trio of the vulnerable*: the widow, the orphan, and the sojourner.[4] I marveled at God as "father to the fatherless."[5]

As I turned to the New Testament, I grew more aware of Jesus' life and teaching on caring for the weak, the vulnerable, and the outcasts. I was also impacted by Paul's commitment to help the weak, and consider the poor, along with the other apostles.[6] James's words riveted me, "Religion that is pure and undefiled before God, the Father, is this: to visit orphans and widows in their affliction."[7] Jesus' words to the religious hypocrites had the same effect: "Woe to you, scribes and Pharisees, hypocrites! For you tithe mint and dill and cumin, and have neglected the weightier matters of the law: justice and mercy and faithfulness."[8] And we made T-shirts with Isaiah's words: "Cease to do evil, learn to do good; seek justice, correct oppression; bring justice to the fatherless, plead the widow's cause."[9]

Please understand, I read these verses before. But I had every reason not to take them at face value. I excused them with theological arguments, like "Liberal theologians do social justice. I don't want to go down that slippery slope." Or, "This is fine for some people to do, but it's not at the heart of what it means to follow Jesus." Or, "That's the Old Testament. That was theocracy." But these pious arguments crumbled as God broke me with His hammer-like Word.

As I worked through these passages of Scripture each day at youth camp, my own preaching convicted me. It was miserable actually. I repented that week of this blind spot in my life and ministry, and vowed to make some changes. I decided as much as possible to simply submit to God's Word, and live in light of it. This decision led me to some questions that would affect my everyday life.

If God is a father to the fatherless, and I am to reflect Him in every way, then doesn't that mean I should care for the fatherless too? If "true religion" involves caring for orphans in their affliction, then what kind of religion am I practicing if it doesn't involve some measure of orphan care? Am I neglecting "the weightier matters" of doing justice and mercy like the Pharisees? Have I turned into a polished professional pastor whose public life is far more impressive than my own personal life?

These questions haunted me. I began to see that in many ways the poorest of the poor were orphans, and there are millions of fatherless kids, not to mention the "functionally fatherless" in our neighborhoods. This reality, coupled with the weight of numerous passages on the subject, led me to repentance and some life-altering decisions.

JESUS AND JUSTICE

Let's get back to Jesus. How did He demonstrate mercy and justice? One of my heroes, John Stott, points us in the right direction, saying:

> What sort of person do we think Jesus Christ is? Have we ever seen him as described in John 11, where first he "snorted" with anger (v. 33, literally) in the face of death (an intrusion into God's good world) and then "wept" (v. 35) over the bereaved? If only we could be like Jesus, *indignant toward evil* and *compassionate toward its victims*.[10]

I have written this book as a recovering Pharisee, who wants to be like Jesus, "indignant toward evil and compassionate toward its victims." If you think you don't need this book, then it's especially for you. I didn't think a study on the poor would impact me either. But maybe you'll recognize some blind spots in your life, like I did.

I'm in an evangelical tribe that believes the Bible, plants churches, and spreads the gospel. I love and support these emphases wholeheartedly. In fact, I planted a church, support my friends serving among unreached people groups, and I teach "expository preaching." But my own tribe struggles with applying the social aspects of the biblical text, a text they view to be inspired and sufficient. Justice ministry is often viewed as an "extra credit option," a "distraction," or something to ignore all together.[11] But those who have a high view of God, His Word, and justification by faith should be leading the way in such ministries. Stott poses some important questions:

> What sort of God do we believe in? Is he concerned exclusively with individual salvation? Or does he have a social conscience? Is he (in the words of Dr. Carl Henry's memorable phrase) "the God of justice and of justification"? How is it that so many of us staunch evangelical people have never seen, let alone faced, the barrage of biblical texts about justice?[12]

We need to face the barrage of biblical texts, and consider how we might practice a life of justice and mercy.

While I'm not a master of everything I'm writing about, it's my desire to practice what I'm writing, not only by myself, but in a community of faith called Imago Dei Church. We planted Imago Dei in Raleigh, North Carolina, in 2011, a church that grew to six hundred in two years. From the beginning, we set out to incorporate mercy and justice ministries within our global missions strategy. Our "PEACE Plan" hangs in our foyer:

P – Plant Churches
E – Evangelize the World
A – Aid the Poor and the Sick
C – Care for the Orphan and the Oppressed
E – Equip Leaders

I don't share this to impress with our church (we have our flaws), or to amaze you with my acronym-making ability (I modified Rick Warren's plan), but to simply share the context from which I'm writing. This really is the heart and soul of our mission. We live it and breathe it.

"ALL THAT IS NECESSARY FOR THE TRIUMPH OF EVIL IS . . ."

You can probably finish this quote, historically attributed to Edmund Burke: "All that is necessary for the triumph of evil is *that good men do nothing.*"[13] Martin Luther King Jr. stated the same idea more emphatically: "He who passively accepts evil is as much involved in it as he who helps to perpetuate it."[14] Others have pointed out that the opposite of love isn't hate, but indifference. Indifference and passivity is a failure to love. We must learn how to love again, which always involves action.

Let me give you a biblical example of indifference and passivity from an obscure passage of Scripture. In 1 Kings 21, the heading in your Bible might say "Naboth's Vineyard." At first glance, this may not interest you, unless you like gardening, grapes, or your name is Naboth. But this passage shouts to us: "Be willing to act on behalf of the oppressed!" Naboth is a righteous Israelite who owns a vineyard. Ahab is the wicked king, or to quote a famous preacher, "the vile human toad who squatted on the throne of Israel."[15] In his greed, Ahab covets Naboth's vineyard and makes him an offer for it. But Naboth refuses to let the land go because he knows the Israelite law. It isn't his to sell. God owns the land. Naboth knows he's simply a steward of it. In response to Naboth's refusal, King Ahab returns to his palace, and pouts like a spoiled child. His evil wife Jezebel can't believe her kingly husband is crying in his pillow. So she proposes a better idea. She writes letters to Naboth's city, with the king's letterhead, and has some men falsely accuse Naboth of blasphemy. They follow her serpent-like scheme, and they stone the innocent man. It's a classic case of injustice and the abuse of power.

What gets my blood boiling in this story isn't simply the wickedness of Ahab and Jezebel. It's the people in Naboth's city. While we don't know all of the details, the biblical writer doesn't give a hint of anyone defending Naboth. Where are the protesters? Where are the men and women crying out for justice? Sure, they were afraid of the king and queen. We can resonate with that. But we can't defend that. All that was necessary for evil to triumph in Naboth's day was for the people *to do nothing.*

Land grabbing remains a serious matter around the world. One of the organizations we partner with is the International Justice Mission. While many know them mainly for their incredible work to fight human trafficking, they also fight to give land back to the vulnerable. In many places, the vulnerable have their land and livelihood violently taken from them. Criminals have been known to come in the middle of the night and cut down a vulnerable widow's crops, burn her house, or even push it over on top of those in the home. Many times the local officials won't help.

I recently watched a story of a Ugandan widow named Grace. Grace's husband became ill and died, leaving her with five children. She then became a victim of property grabbing. She walked twenty-five miles to local officials to get help . . . repeatedly, for two months. But she got nowhere in the process. Of course, she was asked to pay money for the help. It got so bad that she admitted, "I envied death. I became weak by walking so much. I wondered what would happen to my kids if I died." Fortunately, IJM lawyers took up her cause, and advocated for her for nearly three years. After hours of work, she got her land back, and rebuilt her home brick by brick.[16]

Naboth and Grace aren't the only examples of suffering unjustly. Jesus Himself knows what it means for the righteous to suffer. He was the ultimate innocent sufferer. He was also falsely accused and put to death in a kangaroo court even though He was totally sinless.

Naboth's blood cries out for vengeance; but Jesus' blood cries out with forgiveness for the whole world. And the true King promises to return and to execute perfect justice. Evil triumphs for a season, but the King will have the final word when He returns. Until then, His people must avoid passivity, and seek to correct oppression in His name.

MY WIFE'S FIRST TATTOO

People never guess that I'm a pastor and a professor. They typically think I'm in a band, or own a Harley shop or a tattoo parlor. The fact that I have a few tattoos doesn't surprise anyone. But recently, my wife got a tattoo, which surprises people. She's a soft-spoken, diplomatic, professional lady, and a musician. For her thirty-seventh birthday, though, she wanted some ink. She got six words from Micah 6:8: "Do justice, love mercy, walk humbly." The whole verse says this:

> He has told you, O man, what is good; and what does the
> LORD require of you but to do justice, and to love kind-
> ness [mercy], and to walk humbly with your God?

I'm not encouraging getting a tattoo of this verse. But I do want to encourage you to tattoo this verse on your heart.

One Old Testament scholar says of this important verse: "This is the quintessence of the commandments as the prophets understood them."

Another says: "[This verse] is the finest summary of the content of practical religion to be found in the OT." Yet another: "The rabbis who commented on this verse in the early centuries of the Christian era called it a one-line summary of the whole Law."[17]

Think about these claims: the essence of the law, the summary of practical religion found in the Old Testament, and a one-line summary of the whole law. This verse could have been in the mind of Jesus when He spoke of the weightier matters of justice, mercy, and faithfulness.[18]

The Hebrew word translated "kindness," "mercy," or "faithfulness" is, without question, one of the most important words in the Old Testament. It speaks of God's loyal, faithful, covenant-keeping love to His people. God uses it to speak of His own nature.[19] The word *justice* is an action word. It's used to talk about punishing oppressors, as well as protecting and caring for the vulnerable.

These two words, *mercy* and *justice*, obviously go together. Tim Keller says, "To walk with God, then, we must do justice, out of merciful love."[20] I affirm Keller's four-fold description of *doing justice*: (1) Justice is care for the vulnerable; (2) Justice reflects the character of God; (3) Justice is right relationships; and (4) Justice includes generosity.[21]

ORDINARY OR EXTRAORDINARY?

How can we, ordinary people, do Micah 6:8 every day? Do you have to be a lawyer, or a missionary, or a podcasted celebrity preacher? No. You need to walk humbly with God, doing justice out of merciful love for others in every way possible.

While most of the people I highlight in this book aren't extraordinary, some may claim that it's a stretch to call a guy like William Wilberforce "ordinary." After all, he's a Christian hero. Books have been written about him, and recent movies continue to tell his unique story. While acknowledging his uniqueness, I want to hold up the transferable aspects of his life, namely, his communion with God and his faithful labor in a noble cause. Don't distance yourself from him. Identify with him. Learn to commune with the Father like him. He was an ordinary dude.

Several years ago, John MacArthur wrote a book entitled *Twelve Ordinary Men* in which he profiled the disciples. True, these men were extraordinary in one sense, but as MacArthur points out, "They were perfectly ordinary men in every way."[22] These were common guys with various personalities and obvious weaknesses, who responded to an uncommon calling. After a period of training, they were eventually consumed with truth that Jesus vacated a tomb, and because of this event, everything changed. Of course, using ordinary people fits within the nature of the Master, who confounds the wisdom of the age. MacArthur states, "The strategy of Jesus chose typified the kingdom itself."[23] Do you feel too ordinary to be used? Think again! You're just the right candidate! (cf., 1 Cor 1:27–29).

I like the way Steve Timmis and Tim Chester describe the Christian life in their helpful book *Total Church*. The following sentence serves as a good summary of this book: "Most gospel ministry involves *ordinary people* doing *ordinary things* with *gospel intentionality*."[24] Throughout this small book, I want to identify some "ordinary things" that ordinary people like us can do, and if we do them with gospel intentionality (speaking and showing the gospel), then we can make an extraordinary impact.

Consider God's servant Job. As Job reflects on his life, he provides a powerful word picture of an everyday justice kind of life in chapter 29. He says, "I put on righteousness, and it clothed me; my justice was like a robe and a turban."[25] One scholar says, "His clothes witnessed to his complete commitment to justice. Indeed, Job implanted these qualities deep within himself so that they controlled his words and decisions."[26]

Job says that *he wears justice*. He puts it on everyday. He lives with a social conscious. The vulnerable are always on his mind and in his heart. His lifestyle reflects the character of God. The psalmists echoed similar thoughts of everyday justice:

It is well with the man who deals generously and lends;
who conducts his affairs with justice.[27]

Blessed are they who observe justice, who do righteousness *at all times!*[28]

Ordinary is a call to, like Job, wear justice. It's a call to live with a social conscience at all times. It's a call to care for the vulnerable, not merely on mission trips, but in the ordinariness of our days. It's a call to conduct our everyday affairs with honesty and integrity. It's a call to work the character of God deeply into our hearts so that we will care about what God cares about. But it's not a call to be radical; it's a call to be ordinary. It's a call to a new normal.

What does this look like specifically? Consider the verses around Job's word picture. Job highlights the generosity, compassion, mercy, and justice that describe one who wears justice:

> "because I delivered the poor who cried for help,
>> and the fatherless who had none to help him.
> The blessing of him who was about to perish came upon
>> me,
>> and I caused the widow's heart to sing for joy.
> I put on righteousness, and it clothed me;
>> my justice was like a robe and a turban.
> I was eyes to the blind
>> and feet to the lame.
> I was a father to the needy,
>> and I searched out the cause of him whom I did not
>> know.
> I broke the fangs of the unrighteous
>> and made him drop his prey from his teeth."[29]

Job mentions concern for the poor, the fatherless, the dying, the widow, the blind, the lame, the needy, and the oppressed. In chapter 31, he speaks of these same social concerns:

> "If I have withheld anything that the poor desired,
>> or have caused the eyes of the widow to fail,
> or have eaten my morsel alone,
>> and the fatherless has not eaten of it

(for from my youth the fatherless grew up with me as with
    a father,
      and from my mother's womb I guided the widow),
if I have seen anyone perish for lack of clothing,
    or the needy without covering,
if his body has not blessed me,
    and if he was not warmed with the fleece of my sheep,
if I have raised my hand against the fatherless,
    because I saw my help in the gate,
then let my shoulder blade fall from my shoulder,
    and let my arm be broken from its socket. . . .[30]
(the sojourner has not lodged in the street;
I have opened my doors to the traveler)."[31]

These categories mentioned here make up the essential contents
of *Ordinary*: advocacy, hospitality, fatherless ministry, and neighbor
love.

In addition to Job's social concerns, we also find him stressing
sexual purity in chapter 31. He says, "I have made a covenant with my
eyes; how then could I gaze at a virgin?"[32] While sexual purity isn't
a primary focus of this book, we must note the connection between
morality and everyday life. We should never divide our moral and
social lives; this sort of division often enables forms of injustice. For
example, when James tells us to care for orphans and widows in James
1:27, he also says to keep yourself "unstained from the world." A just
life involves a life of *total integrity*, not a focus on either personal
morality or the common good.

Personal morality can actually lead to the common good. For
example, one of the ways you'll actually do justice is by pursuing
sexual purity. If you really want to do something to stop human trafficking, then stop looking at porn. You're perpetuating the problem
of modern-day slavery, and failing to live a just life. Many of the
girls viewed are slaves. When you view pornography, you're helping

destroy their lives—those made in God's image. You're creating more demand, deadening your own soul, and perhaps opening up the door to even more despicable practices. Paul tells us that God's people must live in the light, and shine the light on darkness, not participate in it:

> Therefore do not become partners with them; for at one time you were darkness, but now you are light in the Lord. Walk as children of light (for the fruit of light is found in all that is good and right and true), and try to discern what is pleasing to the Lord. *Take no part in the unfruitful works of darkness, but instead expose them.* For it is shameful even to speak of the things that they do in secret.[33]

Being an *ordinary* Christian can sometimes feel inconsequential. But as we will see in the following chapters, an *ordinary* Christian life most often leads to *extraordinary* consequences. These are the sort of people who turn the world upside down.

CREATION, REDEMPTION, RESTORATION

Why should we bother following Job in this kind of life? While many people know they should care for the poor, few are motivated to do it over a lifetime. What should motivate us? I'll mention three big distinct motivations for doing justice that will be reflected throughout this book.

First, the doctrine of **imago Dei,** or the *image of God*, should compel us to love. If we believe that everyone is made in the image of God, then everyone is worthy of dignity, love, basic human rights, and hearing biblical truth. Those who abuse people made in God's image through enslavement, torture, rape, and grinding poverty, are dehumanizing people and insulting God Himself. Many victims of human trafficking and abuse report how they felt inhumane after being oppressed. Those who believe in the imago Dei should live out their theology through practical acts of love for the oppressed and vulnerable.

Second, remember the doctrine of *redemption*. The Bible records for us the story of God coming to save people. When we were enslaved, He freed us. When we were orphans, He adopted us. When we were sojourners, He welcomed us. When we were widows, Christ became our groom. The mercy and justice of God meet at the cross, where our redemption comes from. We needed His redemption because neither Job nor we can live up to the standard God has set. But One did. Jesus Christ is the ultimate display of a life of righteousness and justice. He wore justice perfectly. Jesus lived the life we couldn't live, and then died the death that we should have died, in order to make us righteous in God's sight. Through repentance and faith in Christ, we are clothed in His righteousness. Now, as believers, we have power to live just lives, and when we fail, we know God won't crush us, for He has already crushed Christ in our place. Now we pursue justice because we love God, and have already been accepted in Him. We want to show mercy. That's what God's redemption has done for us. God has changed our status and our desires. Keller puts it well, "If a person has grasped the meaning of God's grace in his heart, he will do justice."[34]

Third, remember the doctrine of *restoration*. The good news about injustice isn't only that we're making some progress today, though we are. It's that the King of kings will return to restore this broken world, bringing perfect shalom. The kingdom of God has an individual-salvation dimension to it, it's about the realm of God's saving grace; and it also has a socio-future dimension to it, it's about the realm of righteousness, justice, and blessing that is here, but not fully here yet. In the coming Kingdom, will be no more orphans; no more trafficking; no more abuse. This fallen world will give way to glory. Doing justice and mercy is about showing the world what our King is like. It involves *bringing the future into the present*; that is, giving people a taste *now* of what the future will be like *then*. When you welcome the stranger, share the good news among the nations, cultivate diverse friendships, adopt children, or defend the defenseless, you are simply living as the King's people before a watching world. We don't fight the problems of this fallen world as victims, but as victors.

My focus flowing from these motivations is on *people*. You may do justice and mercy through large-scale, political and social transformation like William Wilberforce, who worked to abolish slavery. Or you may do mercy and justice through simple acts like welcoming a foster child. In whatever case, let's do it all in effort to *bless people*. Because *people* are made in God's image, because *people* need redemption, and because *people* will one day dwell with God in the new heavens and the new earth where everything will be finally transformed, we should be seriously interested in how to love our neighbors as ourselves—our orphaned neighbors, our lonely neighbors, our impoverished neighbors, our enslaved neighbors, our racially different neighbors, and our lost neighbors.

WHY ORDINARY?

I was never opposed to orphan care or being generous to the poor. I was just very *indifferent*. Sure, I had a sense of sympathy toward those who were weak and powerless; I saw the pictures and was moved. But I rarely acted. I had to face the fact that sympathy is no substitute for action. My sporadic, momentary experiences of sympathy (for Ukrainian orphans and enslaved girls in the Philippines) didn't help vulnerable children one bit.

Worse yet, I considered myself spiritually mature. I could name a lot of authors and famous preachers, and even knew many of them personally, but I couldn't name an orphan. I began to reevaluate how I evaluate spiritual maturity. Shouldn't we be looking at the life of Jesus, instead of whether or not we are keeping up with the Christian subculture?

Spiritual maturity isn't merely something you do with your mind. It's not about the books you read. It's not about the conferences you attend or speak at. It's about the life you live. It's possible to listen to ten podcasts weekly, and to sing with the hottest bands, and be in four Beth Moore Bible studies, but miss the call to care for the least of these—and all the while live in a deceived state of thinking you're mature.

One of the saddest indications of failure in the area of justice and mercy is our description of those who excel in doing justice. We describe them as radical, as extraordinary. Yet, as we read the Bible together, we find that the Bible treats issues of mercy and justice as anything but extraordinary. Frankly, doing justice is just a normal part of the Christian life.

Ordinary is not a call to be more radical. If anything, it is a call to the contrary. The kingdom of God isn't coming with light shows, and shock and awe, but with lowly acts of service. I want to push back against sensationalism and "rock star Christianity," and help people understand that they can make a powerful impact by practicing ordinary Christianity.

This way of life isn't sexy enough for many in the Christian subculture. They are drawn to mega conferences, mega church pastors, and mega controversies. And that's a problem too. We need Christians focusing on ordinary Christianity—speaking up for the voiceless, caring for the single mom, restoring the broken, bearing burdens, welcoming the functionally fatherless, and speaking the good news to people on a regular basis in order to change the world.

Now let's think together about how we, ordinary people, doing ordinary things, might turn the world upside down.

CHAPTER 1
Neighbor Love
How Justified Sinners Show Compassion in Word and Deed

For the whole law is fulfilled in one word:
"You shall love your neighbor as yourself."

GALATIANS 5:14

A pregnancy crisis center recently contacted us about a particular need. A young teenager got pregnant and had nowhere to turn. Her mother told her that if she didn't choose adoption or choose to abort the baby, then she would be kicked out of her house. One of our pastors, Matt, sent out the word to our church about this need, and an ordinary young couple, Mitch and Amy (pseudonyms), practiced neighbor love in a beautiful way. Amy had been doing a Bible study on the book of James, and that study, coupled with our current series on hospitality, had them asking the question, "How can we be doers of the word and show hospitality to others?" She and Mitch talked that night and decided to respond to Matt's e-mail. The very next day they heard from the pregnancy center! This young girl was about to deliver her baby. She was going to be discharged from the hospital, and be homeless. Mitch and Amy had no idea what to expect, but they opened up their home and knew that God would be with them. As I write, they have hosted this young lady and her new baby for two months.

It's not easy or convenient, but it's definitely made an impact on this teenager and has shown many others what gospel-driven hospitality and neighbor love looks like. Their story makes me weepy-eyed for many reasons, and it reminds me of the story of the Good Samaritan, who simply responded to the need around him.

In a world filled with movies, songs, and stories about false loves, it's refreshing to see what real love looks like. Many confuse love with at least four popular ideas. Millions seek it. Kids dream of it. Artists depict it. Movie buffs crave it. Preachers preach it. Singers sing it. But what is it?

While every generation has its popular love ballads, I remember that the '80s had numerous ones (and a lot of people with really bad hair). In 1984, Foreigner sang, "I Want to Know What Love Is." Tina Turner rocked, "What's Love Got to Do with It?" Stevie Wonder gave us something to say on our rotary-dial telephones with, "I Just Called to Say I Love You." In 1985, Whitney Houston used her amazing voice to sing, "Saving All My Love for You." Kool and the Gang reminded everyone, "love will stand the test of time," with a hit song "Cherish." Whitesnake sang, "Is This Love?" in 1987. That same year, LL Cool J (perhaps my favorite rapper of the era), sang, "I Need Love."

Others could add the most popular love songs of the 1990s and 2000s. There's no small amount of them. If songwriters are the poets and theologians of culture, then one thing is for sure: everyone is interested in love. But many confuse love with at least four popular ideas.

WHAT LOVE IS NOT

Some think love means *tolerance*. Certainly tolerance has a rightful place in culture. It's important in various contexts. In America, one is blessed to freely worship as he or she pleases. However, some believe that you should never disagree or challenge another person's viewpoint. To do so will cause one to be labeled "bigoted" or "narrow-minded." As a Christ-follower, we must not replace truthfulness with tolerance. No one loved like Jesus, yet He was bold and direct. Respect others? Absolutely. Show grace to those who disagree? Yes. Fail to speak the truth in the name of tolerance? No. Paul said it this way, "[Speak] the truth in love."[35] We don't love the world the way Jesus loved the world if we don't call others to repentance. And we should do so in a spirit of brokenness and repentance ourselves. Love doesn't equal tolerance.

Others understand love merely as *eros*. Countless movies, songs, and books are about erotic or sexual love. On a street level, many use love as a magic word to sleep with another person, stripping love of all its nonsexual power. So, if a dude takes a girl out for a movie, and later they do the cupid shuffle together, leaving them hormonally excited, the next move in the "Loser Handbook" is to say the words "I love you." That's code for, "Let's break some commandments." Ladies, don't believe that cat. The type of romantic love that one is made for is *covenant love*. It's the type of love that's talked about in the Bible between God's faithful love for His people; Christ's love for His church; and a husband and wife's love for one another. Love isn't lust.

Many have a *diminished view* of love. We're tempted to use "love" for all kinds of things: "I love pizza." "I love baseball." "I love munchkins from Dunkin' Donuts." In doing this, people have no other word to describe deep, abiding, eternal love. When a teenager says, "I love you" to a girl he just took to the mall, he doesn't usually mean it. He means, "I love you like a munchkin."

Finally, love isn't *sentimentalism*. While one's feelings are very important, we need to remember that love is more than a feeling. Love is more than feeling sorry for someone, or having your emotions stirred by a film or piece of music. Love involves tangible action. When one considers the millions of orphans in the world, or the millions of children being trafficked, or those going without bread today, our sentimentalism isn't helping them. They need someone to act with love.

ORDINARY LOVE: WHAT LOVE IS

So let's try to answer Foreigner's question. How can we tell someone what love is? I believe that the Bible cuts through the fog of confusion on this issue. The apostle John, Jesus' beloved disciple, wrote much about love. Here's what he says:

> By this *we know* love, that he laid down his life for us, and
> we ought to lay down our lives for the brothers.[36]

John says that we don't have to guess about love. If the professor asks you, "What is love?" and you begin listing things on the whiteboard, you can quote 1 John 3:16. What kind of love was this? Jesus' love wasn't simply a mystical love, or a philosophical love, or sentimentalism. Jesus' love was an active love. He didn't merely say He "loved." He demonstrated love. His greatest act of love was at the cross. Paul wrote, "God shows his love for us in that while we were still sinners, Christ died for us."[37]

Therefore, I would define love something like this: *Love involves compassion that leads to action.* Jesus' compassion drove Him to wash His disciples' feet, to serve others, to weep over the city of Jerusalem, and to die as a substitute for sinners. John says it should drive us to lay down our lives for our "brothers."[38] He reminds us also that it's more than *words*, "Little children, we must not love with word or speech, but with truth and action."[39]

God's people are called to care for those in the community of faith with a love that is different from its culturally conditioned counterfeit.[40] But as we scan the whole Bible, we know that Christians are also called to love their neighbor, to love the least of these, and to even love their enemies.[41] Again, Jesus' life and death *exemplifies* such love, and once a person receives salvation in Christ, then the Spirit *empowers* such love. Christ loved the brothers; He loved His neighbor; He loved the least of these; and He loved His enemies. In Jesus, we know what love is; it's the ordinary expression of one neighbor to another.

JESUS' MOST FAMOUS PARABLE

Jesus' most famous parable, typically called "The Parable of the Good Samaritan," is so often misunderstood. Here it is in Luke 10:25–37:

> And behold, a lawyer stood up to put him to the test, saying, "Teacher, what shall I do to inherit eternal life?" He said to him, "What is written in the Law? How do you read it?" And he answered, "You shall love the Lord your God with all your heart and with all your soul and with all your strength and with all your mind, and your neighbor as yourself." And he said to him, "You have answered correctly; do this, and you will live."
>
> But he, desiring to justify himself, said to Jesus, "And who is my neighbor?" Jesus replied, "A man was going down from Jerusalem to Jericho, and he fell among robbers, who stripped him and beat him and departed, leaving him half dead. Now by chance a priest was going down that road, and when he saw him he passed by on the other side. So likewise a Levite, when he came to the place and saw him, passed by on the other side. But a Samaritan, as he journeyed, came to where he was, and when he saw him, he had compassion. He went to him and bound up his wounds, pouring on oil and wine. Then he set him on his own animal and brought him to an inn and took care of him. And the next day he took out two denarii and gave them to the innkeeper, saying, 'Take care of him, and whatever more you spend, I will repay you when I come back.' Which of these three, do you think, proved to be a neighbor to the man who fell among the robbers?" He said, "The one who showed him mercy." And Jesus said to him, "You go, and do likewise."

In this parable, the Samaritan was moved with "compassion," which led him to action. He saw the need of a real human being. He had compassion on him, and made an inconvenient and financial sacrifice. He was committed to helping him in a real way.

After telling this story, Jesus says, "Go and do likewise."[42] It was the Samaritan, not the religious leaders, who was held up as the example to follow.

Simple enough, right? Yes and no. Let's look closer.

While many are familiar with the parable, the context is often ignored (verses 25–28 specifically, but also the surrounding context of Luke's Gospel). As a result, the story is often presented as a mere moral example: Be a Good Samaritan. To be sure, he is a wonderful example. But there's more than example here. Jesus is teaching the gospel.

What one must see in this text is how the gospel is related to good deeds. The order of good deeds and good news is a matter of life and death. Good deeds follow the good news, but good deeds cannot merit eternal life.

Luke tells us that a "Bible Lawyer" asks Jesus this question: "What must I do to inherit eternal life?"[43] It's a good question. It gets echoed throughout films, conversations, and public forums. It's expressed like this in *Pirates of the Caribbean*, "Arr ye fearin' the hereafter?"

Why does this question provoke us? One biblical writer says, "God has put eternity into man's heart."[44] The lawyer is to be commended for his question; however, it seems that his motive isn't right. Luke says that his goal was to "test" Jesus. He may have thought that Jesus had a low view of the law, and he wanted to point it out. But Jesus shows that the lawyer actually doesn't have a high enough view of the law.

THE IMPOSSIBILITY OF ORDINARY LOVE

Religious leaders often sought to trap Jesus, but Jesus actually trapped them. When a different individual tried to ask Jesus about how to have eternal life, known as the Rich Young Ruler,[45] he too received more than what he was anticipating. Jesus told the young ruler to sell everything and give it to the poor. In both stories, Jesus was trying to crush their self-righteousness.

Instead of answering the lawyer's question about inheriting eternal life, Jesus asks him "How do you read it?"[46] Instead of quoting the entire Old Testament, the lawyer summarized it. He quotes Deuteronomy 6:5 ("loving God"), and Leviticus 19:18 ("loving one's neighbor"). To the lawyer's credit, he gave a good answer. These commands are repeated elsewhere in the New Testament, and cited by Jesus.[47] We call these two commandments "the Great Commandments" due to their significance.

But Jesus' interest wasn't in pointing out *the imperative* to love one's neighbor. He wanted to show *the impossibility* of loving one's neighbor 100 percent of the time. Jesus isn't teaching "salvation by roadside assistance." He wants to crush this man's self-righteousness, to expose him of his need for a Savior.

However, instead of humbling himself, the lawyer seeks to "justify himself," asking, "Who is my neighbor?"[48] He seeks a theological loophole. He wants the minimal requirements. Instead of embracing his neighbor, the lawyer wants to philosophize about what "neighbor" means. If you can't keep the commandments, then you might be tempted to redefine them.

From this desire for self-justification, Jesus tells the famous parable, which actually intensifies the point. Jesus crushes the lawyer's self-righteousness, and cuts him to the heart by exposing the lawyer's racism against Samaritans. Jesus says that anyone in need is your neighbor, regardless of race or class. Such weighty instruction—that

one must love their neighbor, anyone in need, including one's enemies—should make one cry out "be merciful to me a sinner."

SALVATION IS A GIFT

That salvation is a gift of grace given by the Savior is taught
throughout the New Testament,[49] and is actually taught in this same
chapter of Luke's Gospel as the parable of The Good Samaritan. In
the beginning of Luke 10, Jesus sends out seventy disciples to do ministry. They come back rejoicing in all that they accomplished.[50] But
Jesus rebuked them saying, "Do not rejoice in this, that the spirits are
subject to you, but rejoice that your names are written in heaven."[51] In
other words, these disciples were to find their greatest happiness and
deepest sense of security in what God had done for them, not in what
they had accomplished for God.

Then, in the very next paragraph of Luke 10 Jesus reiterates
salvation by grace alone saying, "I thank you, Father, Lord of heaven
and earth, that you have hidden these things from the wise and understanding and revealed them to little children; yes, Father, for such was
your gracious will."[52] He then says that "no one knows who the Son is
except the Father, or who the Father is except the Son and anyone to
whom the Son chooses to reveal in him."[53] In other words, salvation
is a gift of God.

If we back up a bit further in Luke's Gospel to chapter 9, we read
an extremely important verse for understanding the Good Samaritan
story, and Luke's entire Gospel. Luke writes that Jesus "set his face
to go to Jerusalem."[54] The rest of Luke's narrative is to be understood
in light of the cross. Jesus isn't setting His face to Jerusalem and then
saying, "You can have eternal life by being nice to your neighbor."
He's going to the cross because no one completely loves God and
neighbor the way the Bible demands. Except one: Jesus Himself! Jesus
lived the life we couldn't live and died the death we should have died.

Luke is showing us that we are saved by grace alone, through faith alone, in Christ crucified alone.

A few chapters later, Luke gives us a story of what this looks like. In Luke 18, two men go pray: a religious professional, and a despised tax collector. Jesus says one of them prayed a self-righteous prayer, "I thank you that I'm not like other men. . . ."[55] But the other "would not even lift up his eyes to heaven, but beat his breast, saying, 'God be merciful to me a sinner!'"[56] Then Jesus tells us who understands the gospel, highlighting the prayer of the tax collector. He says, "I tell you, this man went down to his house justified, rather than the other."[57] Justification is a gift of God's grace, given to all who humbly cry out to Christ in humble repentance.

THE GREAT SAMARITAN

Interestingly, some have pointed out that the ultimate Good Samaritan is Jesus. I'm not sure that Luke intends to communicate that, but it's true. Indeed, Jesus was despised and rejected, like the Samaritan. He acted differently than the religious professionals of the day, caring for the weak and marginalized. He was moved with compassion and, at great cost to Himself, came to save dying individuals. He owed us the exact opposite of mercy, but gave it to us out of His amazing love.

If you have come to Jesus, crying out for mercy, and He has justified you, then you should praise Him for it. If you haven't, then I encourage you to consider the gospel. We can't keep God's command to love our neighbor as ourselves perfectly. But Jesus has kept the Great Commandments perfectly for us. And only Christ can justify us. Only Jesus can make us ordinary citizens of the kingdom of God.

Justification means "just as if I've never sinned" and "just as if I've always obeyed perfectly."[58] Jesus Christ can forgive you entirely, and give you His perfect righteousness.

Justified people stand accepted in Christ. So, don't look to your-self for salvation, but trust in Christ alone. From this acceptance and justified position, we can live in the power of the Holy Spirit to do good to all your neighbors. Tim Keller explains how receiving the good news leads to a life of good deeds:

> Before you can give neighbor love, you need to receive
> it. Only if you see that you have been saved graciously by
> someone who owes you the opposite will you go out into
> the world looking to help absolutely anyone in need.[59]

In other words, justification leads to justice for others. Receive—and give—the neighbor love of the Great Samaritan, and give Him thanks.

GOOD DEEDS FOLLOW

It's a truism that "We are justified by faith alone, but the faith that saves is never alone." Saving faith is an active faith. God's people are about God's business. The Reformer, Martin Luther, put it well:

> Oh, it is a living, busy, active, mighty thing, this faith; and
> so it is impossible for it not to do good works incessantly.
> It does not ask whether there are good works to do, but
> before the question rises; it has already done them, and is
> always at the doing of them. He who does not these works
> is a faithless man.[60]

The believer who has been justified by grace alone should be instinctively engaged in good deeds. The half-brother of Jesus, James, reminds us of three kinds of faith: *dead faith, demonic faith,* and *dynamic faith.* Dead faith simply involves an empty profession of faith, but doesn't give evidence to saving faith. James says that this type of faith is "useless."[61] Demonic faith simply says, "I believe in God." James says that even demons do that.[62] Dynamic faith, however, is that to which Luther referred. It's a faith that functions. James uses the example of Abraham and Rahab to show how true faith leads to real practical obedience to God.[63]

Switching biblical authors, Paul says that while we aren't saved *by* good works, we were saved *for* good works.[64] Spurgeon comments:

> [The Christian] serves his Lord simply out of gratitude;
> he has no salvation to gain, no heaven to lose . . . now, out
> of love to the God who chose him, and who gave so great
> a price for his redemption, he desires to lay out himself
> entirely to his Master's service. . . . The child of God
> works not *for* life, but *from* life; he does not work to be
> saved, he works because he is saved.[65]

What kind of works are ordinary Christians supposed to be doing? A starting point is with the Great Commandment: Love your neighbor as yourself. Simple enough. What does it look like to love our neighbor, or to do what some call "mercy ministry"? Tim Keller says that ministries of mercy involve "meeting felt needs through deeds."[66] Simple enough. Individuals and churches should be sensitive to the needs around them, and seek to meet those needs.

Here's the problem: Not everyone agrees on the nature of or need for mercy ministry! One group promotes social action, but doesn't preach justification by faith alone. It's social ministry with no gospel. This group longs to see the needs of the city met—with absolute sincerity—but for whatever reason, the gospel is either overlooked or avoided. Mercy ministry is service, but lacks proclamation.

Another group proclaims the gospel, but shirks back from social action in fear of compromising truth. The idea of laboring for the good of a lost neighbor seems like a waste of time if agreement on the doctrine of justification is not first reached. It might be confusing to the world, for example, if believers and unbelievers are both trying to serve the poor together by serving meals. For this group, real mercy ministry is proclamation, but lacks concern for the social needs of others.

Let me propose some principles for reconciling that tension.

1. Let's embrace mercy ministry under the shadow of the cross.[67] This point is another way to say we must do both. The kind of mercy ministry advocated by the book of James is one of the Word and of deeds. Just as Jesus talked about loving our neighbor on His way to the cross, let's do mercy ministry under the shadow of the cross. Let's love our neighbor by demonstrating practical love, and let's love our neighbor by declaring the only message that will save. It's really that simple, but others make it difficult by their attitude toward either evangelism or social ministry.

Stop quoting Saint Francis. People fired up about good deeds often quote St. Francis of Assisi, saying, "Preach the gospel and if necessary use words." But this is problematic. Francis probably didn't say it, and more important, it's not true. The gospel must include words. Why? Because the gospel is *an announcement*. *Gospel* means "good news." No newscaster will get on MSNBC or FOX and say, "Tonight, I'm going to bring you the news, and if necessary, I'll use words." They must speak words to give the news.

We must use words. Remember that this parable is given in the context of Jesus' going to Golgotha to pay the penalty for sinners like us. Every story in the Gospels, and in the Bible for that matter, is to be read with Golgotha in view. This message of salvation in the Substitute must be told. Peter said, "He himself bore our sins in his body on the tree."[68] You can't communicate this essential message apart from words.

Sadly, many today want to do mercy and justice ministry without talking about the atonement. But this shouldn't be the case. Mercy ministry is about alleviating suffering. Those who want to alleviate suffering should want to alleviate more than temporary suffering. They should also want to alleviate eternal suffering, which can only come through faith in Christ.

GLOBAL EVANGELISM AS A JUSTICE ISSUE

Often we hear the call to take the gospel of justification by faith alone to the nations. We are often told to do this out of love for the world. That's a good motivation. However, I would also like to point out a different nuance to the notion of love that we've been making throughout this book. Justice is also about love. When it comes to global evangelism, justice says, "It is not right to keep the good news to ourselves when others have never heard it." The gospel is the cure for the worst of all diseases. If we really care about justice ministry, we will really care about taking the cure to the ends of the earth. And, for the record, nearly half the world's people groups live where there is no gospel access. Half. Let that sink in. We need to make this our problem. We need to pray. And we need to go.

But for those who only champion proclamation, and discard mercy ministry, I want to remind them of a few things. The places of greatest poverty and social need are often the places with the greatest need for gospel proclamation also. We don't need to argue over whether we should do word ministry or deed ministry; we simply need to go. When we get there, we should serve them in love and speak to them in love.

The "anti-social ministry" people need to also remember that some can't hear our proclamation until they've been delivered physically from injustice and other forms of suffering. Until we pick them up from the road, they won't hear of the good news. Today, millions are being drugged, sold, and raped multiple times a day in sex trafficking. Do you think they will hear your proclamation? I don't.

This argument reminds me of Exodus 6:9, where we read of Israel's slavery in Egypt. We read, "They did not listen to Moses, because of their broken spirit and harsh slavery." Commenting on this passage, Spurgeon said:

> Some cannot receive Christ because they are so full of anguish, and are so crushed in spirit that they cannot

find strength enough of mind to entertain a hope that by
any possibility salvation can come to them. . . . the mere
struggle to exist exhausted all their energy, and destroyed
all their hope. . . . I do not wonder that a great many are
unable to receive the gospel in this city of ours, because
their struggle for existence is awful. . . . If any of you can
do anything to help the toil-worn workers, I pray you, do
it.[69]

Let's do all we can for the weak to alleviate their present suffering, and let's do all we can to tell them of the glory that is to be
revealed to those who are in Christ. Tell them about the King, who
will usher in a new kingdom of complete shalom, where the lion plays
with the lamb.

THE WAY FORWARD: LOVE PEOPLE

Those who think you must decide between either proclamation
or good deeds puzzle me. I don't think Jesus woke up and asked,
"Should I do ministry of the word, or ministry of deeds today?" It's
a false choice. The same motive for giving a cup of cold water, or to
adopt an orphan, is the same instinct that drives us to proclaim the
gospel: *love*. Jesus put these two together. We must also put them
together.

John Stott points out that the church has historically put the two
together. He says:

It is sadly still the case that some believe that Christians
do not have a social responsibility in this world but only
a commission to evangelize those who have not heard the
gospel. Yet it is evident that in his public ministry Jesus
both "went about . . . teaching . . . and preaching" (Matt.
4:23; 9:35) and "went about doing good and healing" (Acts
10:38). In consequence, "evangelism and social concern

have been intimately related to one another throughout
the history of the church. . . . Christian people have often
engaged in both activities quite unselfconsciously, without
feeling any need to define what they are doing or why."
Our God is a loving God who forgives those who turn to
him in repentance, but he is also a God who desires justice
and asks us, as His people, not only to live justly but to
champion the cause of the poor and the powerless.[70]

So let's cut through all this complexity by learning to simply love
people. Loving our neighbor as ourselves means to love the whole
person, not just the "spiritual" aspects of a person. We aren't gnostics.
We don't believe the physical world is evil. And loving our neighbor
as ourselves doesn't just mean caring for others only "physically." My
friend Russell Moore puts it well:

> Now, there are always going to be those people who want
> to turn the mission simply into the physical maintenance
> of peoples and cultures. On the other hand, there are
> also going to be those people who want to turn to the
> hyper-spiritual and to say, "Let's not be concerned with
> what people eat. Let's not be concerned with the shelter
> that people have. Let's not be concerned with their cul-
> tures and with their communities. Let's simply be con-
> cerned with individual transport from earth to heaven."
> Jesus allows us no such thing. You are to love God and
> you are to love neighbor as self. That means every aspect
> of human existence is being addressed here by the gospel.
> Carl F. H. Henry once spoke of the evangelical tendency
> to speak only of the spiritual aspect of mission—only
> speaking directly to evangelism and not speaking to the
> mercy that people need. This mercy asks the simple
> question, "If I am to love my neighbor as myself, do you
> minister to yourself in only that way?" Do you refuse to

> feed yourself because you have the gospel? Do you refuse
> to clothe yourself because you have the gospel? Do you
> refuse to learn how to disciple your children because you
> have the gospel? No.[71]

In other words, as you purify water systems, tell of the living water in Christ. As you hug the AIDS patient, remind them of the glory of God that will be revealed to the saints. As you ladies care for homeless prostitutes, share how Jesus transformed ladies just like them by His redeeming love. Love your neighbor as you love yourself—your whole self.

In Acts 20, Paul gives a farewell address to the Ephesian elders. He also put preaching the Bible and doing justice together. After describing his preaching of the whole counsel of God, he concludes by saying, "we must help the weak and remember the words of the Lord Jesus, how he himself said, 'It is more blessed to give than to receive.'"[72] Keller comments on this passage saying, "You don't use 'last words' without saying something that is all-important to you. For Paul it was: 'Don't only preach—help the poor.'"[73]

Some worry that "social action is a slippery slope to liberalism." Hear their concern, but don't buy their logic.

I want to ask my friends, "Is it wrong to obey the Great Commandment?" No. Don't deny the social imperative in fear of adopting a social gospel. Simply yield to the Bible and let it shape your heart and life.

Jonathan Edwards, who preached "Sinners in the Hands of an Angry God," was anything but a "liberal progressive." He once said, "Where have we any command in the Bible laid down in stronger terms, and in a more peremptory manner, than the command of giving to the poor."[74] Did you get that? Nothing is clearer in the Bible than loving the poor. His belief never led him down this theoretical slope. You're never moving in the wrong direction by obeying the Great Commandment.

Other evangelicals argue that caring for those in need is the responsibility of *the individual, not the church*. But this is a misunderstanding of the church, and a strange application of the Bible. The church isn't a building you visit, or an event you attend, but a people to which you belong. It's your identity as a Christian. Christianity is personal, but it's not individualistic. It's corporate. The church is about a people, living life together on mission in the name of Jesus. We put the gospel on display not only by how we love each other, but also how we love the world.

Another enemy of neighbor love is *cause-centered Christianity*. It's easy to get excited about a cause, but never actually doing anything for a real person. Today it's popular to put on a wristband advocating for the enslaved, or to wear a T-shirt pressing the need for clean water. That's all fine and good, but remember love isn't sentimentalism, nor is it a cause. Give a name. What desperate neighbor are you loving? Remember, Jesus wanted to know something very specifically in this story, "Who will help *this dying man*?" It's not complex. It's practical. It's possible to discuss job opportunities or poverty without ever doing anything. Whose needs are you meeting with deeds of mercy?

WHAT DOES MERCY MINISTRY LOOK LIKE?

To embrace mercy ministry under the shadow of the cross means to get involved personally. This Samaritan ripped up his schedule, got his hands dirty, gave financially, stayed the night (it seems); he gave love, advocacy, and friendship. Mercy ministry is very broad. It could include, but is not limited to, the following:

Supporting the single mother

Defending vulnerable widows (especially in poor areas of the world)

Caring for orphans

Feeding the hungry

Praying with the dying

Freeing the enslaved

Giving medical care to the diseased

Helping the unemployed

Visiting prisoners

Welcoming sojourners

Counseling the abused

Comforting the grieving

Serving the elderly

Caring for the mentally ill

Tutoring the underprivileged

Ministering to juvenile delinquents

Caring for the disabled

Welcoming internationals

Ministering to the addicted

Aiding victims of disaster

Reforming broken social structures

Doing aftercare for rescued victims of trafficking

Fighting child labor, child pornography, and child prostitution

Seeking racial reconciliation

Bringing the gospel to the spiritually lost

Who should you focus on? I find Jesus' parable helpful for answering this question. This Samaritan cared for the person on his path. I don't think one church can do everything, nor can one person. The question is, who is the dying man in your road? Who has God made you aware of that needs mercy? Such individuals are all around us. They may also be around the world, as we are made aware of global issues. The writer of Proverbs says, "Do not withhold good from those to whom it is due, when it is in your power to do it."[75] We can't do it all, but we can all do something for our neighbors.

2. Let's be motivated by the gospel of grace, not guilt. God cares not only about our deeds; He cares about our motives as well. One may be motivated to do good in order to gain merit before God, or to impress others, or a hundred other reasons. Guilt is often used to get people moving. I hate to admit it, but I've used guilt as well. What

I've discovered is that guilt is not only a great initiator but a poor sustainer. People eventually change the channel. They stop listening. They usually feel despair, or if they are self-righteous, feel prideful because they think they love their neighbor well. Let's motivate, and be motivated, by grace, not by guilt.

We ultimately aren't moved to action by seeing sad pictures, and hearing this: "Look at the big car you drive. How can you let this kid starve while spending all that money on an automobile!" That may change a person for a moment, but it won't produce a life of mercy.

But the gospel melts our hearts. It's the only engine that can empower and sustain a life of mercy ministry. It shows us first how we can't measure up, and then points us to the Redeemer, who receives us, washes us, forgives us, empowers us, and keeps renewing us beside still waters. We will love others well, when we rest in the love of the Redeemer.

An honest Christian reading this book may admit, "I don't love people like I should. How can I grow in my love?" Take note of what Paul says in 2 Corinthians. He says, "The love of Christ controls us."[76] Then he says, "Because we have concluded this: that one has died for all, therefore all have died; and he died for all, that those who live might no longer live for themselves but for him who for their sake died and was raised."[77] Notice that the reason Paul says that Christ's love controls him is because he has reflected upon *the cross of Christ.* The way you grow in your love for others, especially your enemies, is by working the message of the cross deep down into your soul. The more I'm saturated with the love that Christ has had on the ill-deserving, like me, the more loving I become. Paul goes on to say that one of the effects of embracing the message of the cross is that it frees us from our addiction to ourselves. Paul says, "Those who live might no longer live for themselves."[78] Those who are controlled by Christ's love are melted by the message of the cross, freed from self-absorption, and driven to live for the good of others and the glory of the risen Christ. This is a motivation we have to keep coming back to every day.

Later in 2 Corinthians, Paul gives an example of how the gospel fuels mercy ministry. When urging the Corinthians to give generously, he doesn't use guilt. He uses grace instead. He says, "For you know the grace of our Lord Jesus Christ, that though he was rich, yet for your sake he became poor, so that you by his poverty might become rich."[79]

The more one works the grace of Jesus into their hearts, the more generous they will become. Once you realize that you've been forgiven of an infinite debt, you will practice open-handed generosity. A new heart will lead to a new use of money.

The gospel really does change us to care for people in practical ways. Think about this. Luke is known for being the gospel writer who wrote more about caring for the poor and more about hospitality than the other gospel writers. He's the only one who writes of the Parable of the Good Samaritan. But it wasn't because he was more "progressive." He also wrote about justification by grace through faith alone. Luke shows us the relationship between justification by faith and good deeds. The two go together. Grace-saturated people should be mercy-showing and justice-seeking people.

3. Let's remember that mercy ministry radically impacts the world. We don't know what happened to this lawyer. One hopes that the message of Christ changed his heart. Surely, this radical picture of compassion impacted him.

Our broken world needs mercy ministry, and the watching world needs to see others do it. Mercy ministry removes a lot of objections that others have about Christianity. Many think that religion does more harm than good. Certainly, much evil has been done in the name of religion. The world needs to see a true and compelling picture of Christianity.

The Emperor Julian, "the Apostate," in the mid-300s, tried to stop the spread of Christianity. He was angry because it was growing.

He said that a reason for the spread of it was Christians' "charity to the poor." He said, "The impious Galileans not only feed their own poor but ours as well, welcoming them to their agape; they attract them, as children are attracted, with cakes."[80]

Such love was compelling to others. Such ministries of mercy arose from the mercy Christians received in Christ. They put into practice Jesus' words, "Be merciful, even as your Father is merciful."[81]

Let's go and do likewise. Not to earn salvation. But as glad-hearted servants who have received infinite mercy from the Great Samaritan, Jesus Christ.

CHAPTER 2
Kingdom Hospitality
How the King's People Welcome Others

Involvement with people, especially the marginalized, begins with a profound grasp of God's grace.

TIM CHESTER, *A MEAL WITH JESUS*

There is nothing more ordinary than a meal. In preparation for a message on hospitality (Luke 14:12–24), I asked my kids at the dinner table, "What are your all-time favorite meals?" The answers included meals at birthday parties (especially those with piñatas!), Thanksgiving dinners, and Christmas dinners. My wife included a Passover meal that we had with some friends. My top pick was our wedding dinner. I'll never forget the music, the friends, the amazing food, and of course, eating with my new beautiful bride, my dear companion, Kimberly.

What are your all-time favorite meals?

My guess is that the majority of people wouldn't select meals based solely on taste; they would pick meals that involved special company. Friends, family, fun, and good food are ingredients for unforgettable meals. You want these nights to last forever.

Few people would select the burrito they grabbed one night at a Taco Bell drive-thru as their all-time favorite meal, or eating Ramen

Noodles alone as a broke college student, or grabbing a chicken wrap as they scurry to their gate at the Atlanta airport. We long for more. So much more.

How does something as ordinary as a meal become extraordinarily meaningful? Why is it that when a loved one dies in your family, one of the most precious memories you have of them is around the dinner table? Their absence is felt particularly strong when you sit down *without* them. What is this saying to us?

HOSPITALITY AND THE KINGDOM OF GOD

All of these experiences are pointing us toward the kingdom of God. The apostle John tells us of a marriage supper in Revelation 19, in which we enjoy a meal with our King. Christ is the Groom and we are His bride. It's a picture of total satisfaction. Isaiah prophesied about this messianic feast, saying:

> On this mountain the LORD of hosts will make for all
> peoples a feast of rich food, a feast of well-aged wine, of
> rich food full of marrow, of aged wine well refined. . . .
> He will swallow up death forever; and the Lord GOD will
> wipe away tears from all faces.[82]

Think about this vision. The Lord Himself will prepare a meal with the finest of meats and the finest of wines for His people. He will serve the best, and we won't have an ounce of disappointment.

The reason we long for companionship and good food with great friends and family is that we're made for this experience. This life is pointing us to the next life. Unfortunately, too many of us have underdeveloped notions about heaven. Some think it's an endless sing-along. Others have a cartoon concept of heaven, like sitting on a cloud in a diaper playing a harp. Still more have an Eastern idea of heaven. When they think of heaven, they think of an ethereal realm of disembodied spirits.

Let's think again. Think new heaven and new earth, with our real, glorified bodies, with Jesus, and all His people, feasting and rejoicing in the grace of God.

Don't get me wrong, we're not *only* going to feast in heaven, but one of the pictures that we should see is this idea of a messianic banquet. Jesus told a parable saying that all are invited to His banquet, yet sadly many decline the invitation because other things are more important.[83] How kind of the King to invite us to His party!

WHAT IS HOSPITALITY?

We need to see hospitality through the lens of Scripture in order to understand it rightly and find motivation to do it faithfully. Hospitality doesn't mean *entertaining* people. "Entertaining" is often about impressing others; hospitality is about serving others. Entertaining is often about the host; hospitality is about the guests. Entertaining is often shallow and superficial; hospitality is about depth and authenticity.

Not only should we distinguish hospitality from entertaining, but we should also distinguish it from *fellowship*. Generally speaking, fellowship happens among believers in biblical community (which we need). But *hospitality* literally means, "love for strangers." Hospitality is what we extend to outsiders, strangers, and those in physical and spiritual need.

To qualify, I don't think you need to worry if your hospitality has a mixture of believers and unbelievers; of needy and not-so-needy people. For it seems that Jesus regularly had a mixture of people around Him. My point is that we must have an open heart/home toward people that extends beyond what's comfortable, culturally normal, and exclusive. Jesus' hospitality was countercultural and inclusive in that He hung out with riffraff and the needy, and He certainty didn't try to show off His fine china. For Jesus, the table was a place for friendship, welcome, gospel communication, and mission. We need to follow His example and use the table and our homes to put the gospel on display.

Hospitality is a culturally appropriate way to do faithful evangelism, and a practical way to do ordinary mercy and justice. It's also biblical imperative. It isn't limited to a single verse, but is woven throughout the story line of Scripture. As we seek to elevate our view of hospitality, consider three exhortations: (1) Opening Our Bibles; (2) Opening Our Hearts; and (3) Opening Our Doors.

Opening Our Bibles

Hospitality Revealed in the Biblical Story Line: One could tell the story of Scripture through the theme of hospitality. In the garden, God provided a home and provision for Adam and Eve, but they rebelled against Him. Despite their sin, God graciously *clothed them* by making garments of animal skins.[84] Keller calls this the first act of mercy ministry.[85] While it certainly has a spiritual dynamic of covering our sin, it shows more than that since this was a physical provision also. Derek Kidner comments on it, saying, "Social action could not have had an earlier or more exalted inauguration."[86]

God the host not only provided food and clothing for our first parents, but later in the book of Exodus He provided miraculous food and water for His people as they wandered in the wilderness. During this forty-year journey, their clothes and sandals never wore out either![87] Additionally, the Exodus was to be remembered through the Passover meal. The Israelites would taste the grace of God, and reflect upon His salvation in this table experience.

The story goes on. God promises His people that He will take them to "a land flowing with milk and honey."[88] God hosts His people and gives them an enjoyable home.

Fast-forward to the New Testament. Jesus appears, and is constantly eating with people, and even gets labeled as "a glutton and a drunkard, a friend of tax collectors and sinners!"[89] He even eats in the homes of the hated tax collectors, like Levi and Zacchaeus.

The church is established next, and the first worship gatherings took place in homes. They welcomed others, as Christ welcomed them.[90] Hospitality was at the heart of the early church. (I often tell our church-planting students that what they're about to do is attempt to practice hospitality well.)

Finally, why does Paul rebuke Peter to his face? It was because Peter refused to eat with Gentiles, which was more than mere rudeness; it was "not in step with the truth of the gospel."[91] Paul also scolded the Corinthians because of their unacceptable elitism around the Lord's Supper.[92] Further, exhortations to practice hospitality are also scattered through the New Testament, as we've already seen in the marriage supper of the Lamb.[93]

Hospitality Displayed—The Old Testament: So, in Scripture we find God welcoming, feeding, clothing, protecting, befriending, and nourishing people. This is the basis for Christian hospitality. Righteous people follow the Righteous One in every way, including hospitality. The writer of Leviticus tells us of this all-important basis for kingdom hospitality:

> "When a stranger sojourns with you in your land, you
> shall not do him wrong. You shall treat the stranger who
> sojourns with you as the native among you, and you shall
> love him as yourself, *for you were strangers in the land of
> Egypt:* I am the LORD your God."[94]

God tells His people that they should welcome the stranger because that's what He did for them. God's hospitality was the basis for their hospitality.

God's welcoming character is beautifully described in Isaiah 55:1: "Come, everyone who thirsts, come to the waters; and he who has no money, come, buy and eat! Come, buy wine and milk without money and without price." Jesus also gives a similar invitation in the New Testament: "Come to me" (Matt. 11:28). Jesus took on flesh, and entered into culture. He went out, and invited others in.

Consider a few servants who display God-glorifying hospitality in Scripture. In Genesis 18, Abraham entertains three guests, one of whom is the Lord! Joseph welcomes and graciously cares for his brothers, and others, during a famine.[95] Righteous Job claims, "the sojourner has not lodged in the street; I have opened my doors to the traveler."[96] Rahab demonstrates hospitality, offering protection and lodging to Israelite spies in Joshua 2, and demonstrating her loyalty to the God of Israel.[97] In the book of Ruth, we see a "little redeemer" in Boaz, who feeds the hungry at his table.[98] Abigail provides hospitality to David and his men in 1 Samuel 25. The widow of Zarephath provides for Elijah in 1 Kings 17, through God's unending supply of flour and oil. Nehemiah also shows us a picture of the hospitality of a leader, as he provides for 150 men at his table, eating delightful food prepared at his own expense.[99]

My favorite Old Testament example is in the kindness of David, who brings a lame man named Mephibosheth to his table; a beautiful picture of Christ our King inviting us to His table. Mephibosheth expresses the humility of a grace-receiver: "And he paid homage and said, 'What is your servant, that you should show regard for a dead dog such as I?'"[100] Despite his unworthiness, David welcomed him. The writer concludes: "So Mephibosheth ate at David's table, like one of the king's sons. . . . So Mephibosheth lived in Jerusalem, for he ate always at the king's table. Now he was lame in both his feet."[101] None of us deserve the King's grace either. How should we respond to the immeasurable kindness of Jesus? With humble hearts, and generous hospitality toward the lonely, the broken, and the needy.

Hospitality Displayed—The New Testament: When we get to the New Testament, God's people are urged to continue this legacy of caring for strangers. When Jesus sent His twelve apostles out to minister in Matthew 10:9–11, He built hospitality into the mission. He emphasizes its importance saying, "Whoever receives you receives me, and whoever receives me receives him who sent me."[102]

Interestingly, one of the qualifications for pastors is "hospitality."[103] Think about this. If a guy doesn't show hospitality, he's unqualified to serve as pastor. I don't think I've ever heard of a pastoral candidate being asked this question in any serious way. Some churches have guys "preach in view of a call" before they vote on him. But I think a more biblical approach is "live in view of a call." Strangely, I've heard pastors bragging about never having a church member in their home. How foreign such "non-hospitality" is to the New Testament. Pastors should be leading the church in showing hospitality, not neglecting to practice it.

Passages like 1 Peter 4:9 and Romans 12:13 exhort all Christians to welcome others. Peter adds that we must do so "without grumbling." God didn't "grumble" when He welcomed us. We should practice it with Christlike joy. The author of Hebrews says something amazing about hospitality, "Do not neglect to show hospitality to strangers, for thereby some have entertained angels unawares."[104] You never know whom you might entertain! Corporately, James rebukes the church for not showing hospitality to the poor in their corporate gathering. Because of this sin, he called into question the integrity of their faith.[105]

Keller points out that Christianity spread in the first century through extended household (*oikos*) evangelism done informally by Christians. He says: "The home could be used for systematic teaching and instruction (Acts 5:42), planned presentations of the gospel to friends and neighbors (Acts 10:22), prayer meetings (Acts 12:12), impromptu evangelistic gatherings (Acts 16:32), follow-up sessions with inquiries (Acts 18:26), evenings devoted to instruction and prayer (Acts 20:7), and fellowship (Acts 21:7)."[106] The early church used their home in remarkably effective and gracious ways.

Resist the temptation of thinking you are too "introverted" for hospitality. This really has nothing to do with personality types, or whether or not you enjoy having company over for dinner. We must see it as a biblical pattern, practiced among all types of God's people—who have all types of personalities. My friend Steve Timmis writes and speaks on the centrality of living in community regularly. Yet, he's a self-professed introvert. His colleague, Tim Chester, has written on hospitality (noted below), yet Steve claims Tim is even more introverted than he is! These men write on community and hospitality, and practice these things, not because they are always "the life of the party," but because they see these things clearly taught in the Bible. You can be an introvert and practice hospitality.

Hospitality Taught and Exemplified by Jesus: Many don't see how much Jesus taught and exemplified hospitality. Jesus ate with sinners throughout His earthly ministry.[107] He received children gladly.[108] He taught us to invite the lowly to parties[109] and to welcome strangers.[110] He prepared breakfast for His wayward disciples, including Peter who had betrayed Him.[111] He ate with the Emmaus disciples after His resurrection.[112] Before His departure, He said He was going to "prepare a place" for His people.[113] Jesus also instituted the Lord's Supper, giving new meaning to the Passover meal, and told us that He will drink it again with us when "the kingdom of God comes."[114]

Jesus' miracles were sneak previews of the kingdom of God to come. In the coming kingdom, there will be no demon-possessed men, no storms to calm, no sicknesses to cure, and no tears of the bereaved to wipe. Each time Jesus performed a miracle, He gave us a taste of what's coming. His first miracle was significantly at a wedding party. The King gave us a glimpse of the ultimate party to come. Happiness, joy, fellowship, and sweet communion with the King awaits His bride.

The promise of enjoying Jesus' glorious kingdom is made possible by His gracious provision. Paul tells us that we were formerly "strangers . . . having no hope and without God in the world"[115] but then adds the good news: "But now in Christ Jesus you who once were far off *have been brought near* by the blood of Christ."[116] Christ came out to us, to bring us in to the family, at great sacrifice and cost. Now we enjoy the unspeakable privileges of the King's hospitality.

The question that we must ask ourselves is whether or not we're practicing Jesus-like ministry. Many Christians see Jesus as a personal moral example (and rightly so), but not as a social example. But why not? When you become a Christian, your social life, how you interact with others, should change also. Do you have a reputation for hanging out with shady company for the purpose of showing them grace? Don't get me wrong. I'm not advocating a cavalier spirit, and certainly not condoning sin. But I'm definitely advocating Jesus-like ministry. Jesus was separated from sin, but never isolated from people. And He definitely wasn't the incarnate kill-joy. Sinners loved being with Jesus. The poor and vulnerable found hope in Him. It was the religious neatniks that got upset with Him. What about you? Does your social life look like His?

In his book *Eating Your Way through Luke's Gospel*, Robert Karris says, "In Luke's Gospel, Jesus is either going to a meal, at a meal, or coming from a meal."[117] Luke gives particular attention to Jesus' table ministry. Tim Chester reflects on this in *A Meal with Jesus*, as he looks at six particular chapters in Luke (5; 7; 9; 14; 22; 24).[118] He poses an interesting question during the introduction, "How would you complete this sentence: The Son of Man came . . ."? Many Christians would answer (1) "The Son of Man came not to be served but to serve, and to give his life as a ransom for many,"[119] and (2) "The Son of Man came to seek and to save the lost."[120] That's correct. But Luke also adds "The Son of Man has come *eating and drinking*."[121] Chester writes: "The first two are statements of purpose. . . . The third statement is a statement of method. . . . His mission strategy was a long meal stretching into the evening. He did evangelism and discipleship 'round a table with some grilled fish, a loaf of bread, and a pitcher of wine."[122]

Following Jesus includes following His practice of hospitality—joyous, authentic, generous, countercultural, and hope-filled hospitality. When Jesus says, "Come follow me," He isn't calling us to offer a class or start a program, but to follow His way of life. And that way includes opening up our homes and lives to others. But before we'll do this, we must open our hearts.

Opening Our Hearts

If we aren't showing hospitality, we must ask "Why not?" At the end of the day, it's a heart issue. The goal is to open our hearts to people, not merely pass the potatoes. The reason our hearts aren't opened to people is because our hearts are idol factories. Therefore, to follow Jesus in this way, we need to put five things to death.

Death to Pride: Perhaps the most radical (radical to us, ordinary to Him, ordinary in the Kingdom) thing Jesus said about showing hospitality is found in Luke 14:12–14. Jesus provides this instruction over a meal with the Pharisees. They probably never invited Him back since He offended everyone at the table.

The religious leaders didn't invite Jesus to the table to show Him grace, but to trap Him theologically. However, Jesus exposes their cold hearts, pointing out how they love to twist the law to protect their selfish lifestyle. His response to their Sabbath question leaves them speechless.

But Jesus also exposes the pride of *the guests* of the party, who want seats of honor, and desire praise from people. Then Jesus gives the axiom of the Kingdom:

> "For everyone who exalts himself will be humbled, and he who humbles himself will be exalted."[123]

The ordinary way of the Kingdom is the way of humility, not self-glorification.

As Jesus is at the table, He looks around and proceeds to tell the religious leaders what's wrong with their party. He says that one way you live out kingdom humility is by practicing gracious, countercultural hospitality.

So, He's already rebuked the guests, and now He rebukes *the hosts*:

He said also to the man who had invited him, "When you give a dinner or a banquet, do not invite your friends or your brothers or your relatives or rich neighbors, lest they also invite you in return and you be repaid. But when you give a feast, invite the poor, the crippled, the lame, the blind, and you will be blessed, because they cannot repay you. For you will be repaid at the resurrection of the just."[124]

How's that for rocking someone's world? If you're going to have a party, good. Just remember that you should give preference to the poor.

Was Jesus too extreme? I don't think so. This has always been God's desire. Hundreds of years earlier, God rebuked His people for their failure to extend such grace through the prophet Isaiah:

"Is not this the fast that I choose:
    to loose the bonds of wickedness,
    to undo the straps of the yoke,
to let the oppressed go free,
    and to break every yoke?
Is it not to share your bread with the hungry
    and bring the homeless poor into your house;
when you see the naked, to cover him,
    and not to hide yourself from your own flesh?"[125]

Isaiah confronts the same type of religious hypocrisy that Jesus confronted in Luke 14. Lots of people were doing religious activities, like fasting, but they weren't showing grace of God to the least of these. The fact that God's preferences are counter to our own, that we view them as radical or extreme, ought to cause us to question what is ordinary on earth in light of what is ordinary in heaven. Our outrage at God's preference for the least of these should be the source of our deepest lament.

To clarify, Jesus isn't opposed to you spending time with friends and family. He accepted invitations to His friends' homes regularly. We also see the early church fellowshipping together constantly.[126] And Jesus told us that the world would know we belong to Him by how we love one another[127]—which implies we need to be with one another.

But don't weaken what Jesus says. Jesus is saying give preference to the poor and vulnerable. If Jesus walked into our parties, banquets, or holiday dinners, I can imagine Him saying, "Great food. Great party. But where are the single moms? Where are the orphans? Where are the special needs children? Where's that snotty-nosed kid down the street, whose dad is imprisoned and his mom is on crack?" We ought to pray, with Jesus, like He did in Matthew 6:10, "Your kingdom come, Your will be done, on earth as it is in heaven."

John Newton, who knew a few things about amazing grace, was passionate about kingdom hospitality. He said of Luke 14:12–14: "One would almost think that Luke 14:12–14 was not considered part of God's Word . . . nor has any part of Jesus' teaching been more neglected by his own people."[128]

We must collapse the distance between the marginalized and us. Otherwise, we're no different from the Pharisees. How much of the Christian culture is built on climbing the ladder of success? How much of our social practices is built on self-glorification? We simply baptize secular social practices, and as a result have a witness that isn't compelling to the outside world.

We must kill pride, and replace it with a heart of humility. We do this by working the gospel deeply into our hearts. When you realize that you were the poor, bringing nothing to the table when Jesus invited you, then it changes your view of the poor. When you realize that you were the crippled, unable to come to God when He brought you in, then it changes the way you think about the weak. Pharisees don't understand grace. They're often mad, self-righteous, and elitist.

Grace-driven people are happy, humble, and hospitable to the poor and weak.

Death to Paybacks: Another problem that people have with showing generous hospitality is that our sinful hearts want paid back for everything. Much of our social life is built around reciprocity. "If I do this, then will you do that?" But Jesus says that we should invite the least of these "because they cannot repay you."[129] He reminds us that our reward is elsewhere, saying, "you will be blessed" and "you will be repaid at the resurrection of the just."[130]

Jesus tells us elsewhere that if you try to do everything out of the law of return, then we're no different than unbelievers.[131] Instead we must give expecting nothing in return, remembering that our reward is heaven. He says: "Be merciful, even as your Father is merciful."[132]

Hospitality is war. It's not the path of least resistance. Because of this reality, you better have some deeper, more sustainable motivations for doing it. God-centered motives like longing to glorify the mercy of the Father, living for another reward, and delighting to obey God's Word satisfies and sustains the hearts of disciples.

I often hear people talking about adoption in romantic ways. They wrongly think that a child "will fill the hole in their heart." I want to tell such prospective parents that they should get a dog instead of a child. Chances are, if you adopt children, do foster care, or simply welcome that functionally fatherless girl down the street, then you probably won't hear sweet, soft-playing music in the background.

You should play *Gladiator* music instead. It will be a struggle probably. You might sleep with one eye opened for a while. But remember, we don't care for children because of what we can get. We do it because we're citizens of the kingdom of God, and He calls us to love our neighbors as ourselves. We do it to show the world what our King is like, and what He has done for us. And if we have any longing for reward, we need to remember that it won't ultimately come in this life, but in the next.

To practice hospitality, we must die to reciprocity. Our guests may never say, "Thanks." They may eat all our food. They may stain our carpet. They may make us weep with grief. That's okay. We're doing this out of love for the person, because we value eternity more than this passing life, because we're simply stewards of God's provisions, and because we love the King.

If you live this way, you'll begin to understand the nature of grace in a powerful way. Paul Zahl says, "Grace is love that seeks you out when you have nothing to give in return."[133] That's how Jesus has loved us. And that's how we're to love the world. Invite others in, seeking nothing in return. Work Jesus' grace into your heart deeply that you may work it out on others similarly.

Death to Sensationalism: Christians often gravitate to "the extraordinary." Of course, seeing lives changed by the gospel is extraordinary to us, but many go from event to event, program to program, trying to quench their sensationalistic appetites. But mission usually doesn't involve doing sensational acts; it involves simple, ordinary acts done with a heart of love.

People often come to our church and ask, "How can I get plugged in?" This question is sometimes another way of asking, "What program can I get involved with, or what kind of events do you all have?" But we don't have programs. I'm not opposed to programs, for there's nothing wrong with them. But many confuse mission for busyness. My typical response is this: "Eat with lots of people this week." They often have a puzzled look. I gently tell them that we don't want a lot of programs during the week because we want people to live out this mission during the week.

At our church in Raleigh, we've adopted the quote I alluded to in the introduction from Chester and Timmis as our posture for mission. Here it is again:

> Most gospel ministry involves *ordinary people doing ordinary things* with gospel intentionality.[134]

In other words, mission isn't always astonishing. It might look like a barbecue, or a neighborhood basketball game, or going grocery shopping for your neighbor. But these ordinary things can have extraordinary effects. That's why international missionaries rejoice when a local non-believer comes to their home for dinner. That's a big deal. We need to adopt this same missionary posture. What do international missionaries do? They serve the poor, and they evangelize people, and often one or both involves eating with people, or serving food to them. It's a lot like the ministry of Jesus. He didn't run programs or start institutions. He ate with people.

I love how Paul says to the Thessalonians, "We were ready to share with you not only the gospel of God but also our own selves."[135] For some, evangelism is gospel with no life—megaphone preaching, handing out tracts, or street evangelism. For others, evangelism is life with no gospel. They equate doing lunch with doing mission. But Paul gives us a nice pattern here: Live life among others, as we speak the gospel to them. Hospitality is one way to do this.

Some assume hospitality is "too small" for them. Big shots might think that it's a complete waste of time. But it's actually the wisest investment of your time. What's more important than caring for people made in God's image, especially the poor and the weak, and sharing the most important message in the entire world with them? Further, Jesus tells us that eternal rewards are in view when it comes to inviting others to our parties. We have extraordinary motives for doing ordinary mission.

On a practical level, we need to die to the pressure of having sensational entertainment. Many fear that they can't do hospitality because they don't have a big enough home, or they can't serve a rich enough meal. But remember again, hospitality isn't entertaining. Entertaining is often about showing off. Hospitality is about showing grace. Serve your guests the best you can, but remember the focus is on welcoming and loving Zacchaeus and Levi, the prostitute and the orphan, not whether you serve them a filet or a hot dog. Don't let the financial cost rob you of the duty and blessing of hospitality.

Death to Partiality: Our refusal to open our doors often comes from a refusal to open our hearts to those who don't look like us. But the Christ-follower should celebrate diversity, not despise it. One of the most beautiful displays of the gospel is when you hang out with people that make others wonder, "Why is he with that guy?" Jesus received the same questions. People didn't invite the poor to parties. They served them out the back door. Jews didn't hang out with Samaritans, but Jesus was willing to share the same cup with a shady lady in John 4.

In encouraging you to practice hospitality, I'm encouraging you to learn how to befriend people who aren't like you. You won't show hospitality if you don't like people, and they don't like you. Jesus was a "friend of sinners."[136] He attracted all sorts of people, and they loved His company, even though He often spoke hard truth to them.

If you don't have any friends that are of a different race, age, or economic status, then ask yourself, "Why not?" Is it impossible because of your context, or do you have a heart problem? Many times churches champion diversity, and that's a good thing. But we need more than a few diverse people on a stage singing songs. We need diverse *friends* who watch *Monday Night Football* at our house. Diverse friends who put their feet up on our furniture and open our fridge. We need to have a meal with the homosexual in order to listen to her and share the glory of God's truth and love.

The first step in overcoming your prejudices toward someone of a different, race, class, part of the nation, or political party, is to admit you have prejudices. Remember that the gospel transcends these boundaries. Remember Jesus loved us when we were unlovely. Remember that Jesus loves diversity, and that heaven will be populated with every tribe and tongue. Practice now a foretaste of what we will enjoy then.

This way of life may sound like youthful zeal or impractical, but if it does, could it be because we've allowed the culture to shape our views more than the gospel? Would others call you "a friend of sinners"? If not, then perhaps you should examine your heart. Our social life is illustrating how much we look like Jesus, and how well we understand the kingdom of God.

Death to Self-Indulgence: We must kill this idea, "My home is my refuge." I often hear people say that. It's idolatry. Jesus is our refuge. We need to open our homes to people.

When you replace *stewardship* for *ownership* you won't practice hospitality.[137] The Christian knows he or she owns nothing. We're stewards of God's possessions, including our homes. The question is not "How much money should I give to advance the Kingdom?" but "How much of God's money should I keep for myself?" And not, "What's the least I can do for people?" But "How many people can I possibly have in the home God provided, and how many people can I serve with God's resources?"

It's not a sin to have a big home. It's a great blessing, and a wonderful tool for loving a broken world. Do you view your home as "the king in his castle," building a moat in order to keep people out? Or are you saying, "My King is Jesus, all may enter in!"

Jesus is better than any comfort you have. Believe that. You don't need a bigger TV and a more comfortable recliner in your "mancave." You need a bigger front door, and more seats filled around the table. Rest in Jesus, as you pour yourself out for the physically and spiritually needy.

Opening Our Doors

Allow me to conclude the chapter by providing some practical ways to do kingdom hospitality with faithfulness and grace. While we should always be ready to open our doors to traveling missionaries, for hosting small group Bible studies, and for hosting our families for extended periods of time, allow me to challenge you beyond these noble practices.

Foster Care: In the next chapter, I'll talk about orphan care more specifically, but for now consider foster care. Today I met with a lady who started a nonprofit to help American foster-care children. I learned that on any given day there are more than 450,000 children in the U.S. Foster Care system. More than 100,000 are waiting to be adopted. It's not uncommon for a child to travel through five or more homes. And get this: Each year, nearly 30,000 children will turn eighteen and age out of the Foster Care System with only a check for $500! Because $500 won't last long, and because these kids have no where to go, it's not surprising that many foster kids end up in a life of crime, prostitution, or gang life.

Believers should be asking, "Why shouldn't I do foster care?" What's keeping you from it? It can't be the financial cost. It's free, and it comes with many financial benefits, like college tuition and monthly stipends. Sure, it's challenging, but think about these kids. They've been tossed around from home to home, locked in closets, shut out of the house, and physically abused; and often have a depressed look of hopelessness. They're also vulnerable to abuse and exploitation. Do you not have room at the table for a foster child? If it's impossible for you to foster, then what can you do to promote foster care? Can you contact the local agencies and see what needs they have? Can your church begin pursuing possible ways to promote foster care in the local church? Are there other ways you can show hospitality to at-risk children?[138]

Aftercare: Often when we hear about human trafficking, we feel overwhelmed and disconnected because the problem is so vast and it seems like a job for politicians, law enforcement, or lawyers. While we certainly need Wilberforce-like servants in these arenas, there are other wonderful ways you can help. One way is aftercare.

When girls are rescued from sex trafficking, we can only imagine the shame and brokenness they feel. What do they need? Among other things, they need friendship, love, the good news of Jesus, and a local church that does community well.

Over the past year, I've seen the blessing of having a community of faith pour into two girls that were rescued from human trafficking. They were placed in a local aftercare facility. Some of the leaders brought these girls to corporate worship, and they were incorporated into our faith community. On several occasions, they've had dinner at our house. In an effort to give relief to their house leaders, they've also stayed overnight at our house on a few occasions. These girls, and others like them, need love, and they need to see what a healthy family looks like.

Are there any aftercare facilities in your area? Would you consider contacting them and asking how you can help? Perhaps you would consider starting an aftercare facility. We're in the early stages of doing this as a church right now. We're praying for a facility, the finances, and the workers. In Haiti, we're working with a terrific organization called Help One Now, and they're doing victim aftercare. They've built several little homes for girls who have been trafficked across the border of Haiti into the Dominican Republic. We need aftercare facilities locally and globally.

Transitional Assistance: Along with these ministries, various forms of transitional assistance remain a great need. Foster-care children and aged-out orphans have nowhere to go. They need jobs. They need community. Some are told lies and promised jobs, but are kidnapped, abused, and sold. I have friends who have started business in impoverished countries for the purpose of providing a place of employment for orphans who have aged out of orphanages. This remains one of the great needs in orphan care.

Other forms of transitional assistance include serving prisoners who have exited the prison system. As with all forms of hospitality, one needs to use wisdom, and this is certainly the case. But don't let fear keep you from serving the prisoner.

Steve Timmis told me of a time in which he invited a former prisoner to stay at his house for a few weeks. He set guidelines. This guest could never be at their home when the family was away, for example. Timmis even had his daughter put her dresser in front of her door at night. Despite the possibility of danger, he welcomed this man and tried to help him get on his feet. If you aren't ready for this, then you might consider volunteering at a halfway house. These places often need volunteers to serve former prisoners who are transitioning.

Hosting Internationals: Some report that nearly 80 percent of the 500,000 international students never set foot in an American home.[139] Are we really that inhospitable as a culture? Some institutions are trying to correct this unacceptable reality. They are seeking to reach out to locals, encouraging them to invite international students over for dinner. Have you looked into this personally? Do you have a school in your area with international students? Does the school already have an organization dedicated to serving internationals? Perhaps you could contact them and see what ways you could serve. We've served Thanksgiving dinner to internationals at NC State. We've sought to invite many to our homes for dinner. It's always an incredible experience.

In addition to serving international students, you may also have opportunity to serve international refugees. Recently, one of our small groups embraced a family of refugees from Baghdad. The group leader was made aware of the need through the World Relief organization. So the group went to the airport and greeted a dad, mom, and three kids (who spoke no English). These refugees, like others, need furniture, ESL training, transportation, and many other practical necessities. You or a group may consider serving refugees in this way too. What a wonderful way to welcome the sojourner.

Other Acts of Neighbor Love: Finally, there are a number of ways to show hospitality locally. You should also host the elderly, or in some cases, go visit them. Regular visits to the elderly, and to the widow, are wonderful ways to show neighbor love and to live out God's Word.

You should also consider ways to serve and love veterans, and those with mental and physical needs. I know of one church that does a prom every year for special needs kids.

Your local police force is another group that you should consider serving. They need to know that people in the church care, and that God's people are praying for them. In addition to this, the church will be made aware of several needs in the community through interacting with them.

You might also consider doing a block party in a difficult part of town. When I was in New Orleans, we cooked a huge pot of red beans and rice and a bunch of us went into one of the roughest public housing developments in the city. Kids came from everywhere. I remember one kid named Anthony ran up and jumped in my arms saying, "Give me a nickel." I gave him a nickel. Then he said, "Give me another nickel, that nickel's dirty!" After going through all my nickels, we played ball until it was dark. As our team was leaving the area, we went back to our SUV. The kids followed us all the way there, and were hanging on the vehicle, not wanting us to leave. As we drove back to our dorms, we passed several church buildings. I just wondered how much was being done for these kids. I prayed for the church to get out of the pews and get into the projects more and more.

There are a hundred other ways to practice hospitality for the good of your neighbors. Our small group just did a chili cook-off for the purpose of reaching out to our friends and neighbors. Over fifty people showed up at my house. It was a fun evening of tasting various recipes and meeting new folks.

Consider using occasions to practice hospitality: birthday parties, housewarming parties, sporting events, or seasonal events (Thanksgiving dinner, Fourth of July celebration, or Christmas dinner). Make up a reason. Have a board-game night, a movie night, or a can-jam tournament. Don't underestimate the power of inviting your neighbors to do ordinary things with you, as you seek to show and share the gospel in a natural and authentic way.

As you bow your head for your next meal, perhaps you could utter this prayer to keep you mindful of the broken world around us: "Father, we thank You for this meal in a world that's hungry. We thank You for friends in a world that's lonely. We thank You for the light of Christ in a world that's in darkness. In Jesus' name, Amen." May God fill us with sensitivity and love, and may we fill our homes with Mephibosheths. And when He does, look at your guest, and remember the King's words:

> "For I was hungry and you gave me food, I was thirsty and
> you gave me drink, I was a stranger and you welcomed
> me, I was naked and you clothed me, I was sick and you
> visited me, I was in prison and you came to me . . . as you
> did it to one of the least of these my brothers, you did it
> to me."[140]

When you see the King, you won't regret having practiced kingdom hospitality.

CHAPTER 3
Care for the Vulnerable
How the Father's Children Love the Fatherless

"I delivered the poor who cried for help,
and the fatherless who had none to help him."

JOB 29:12

Kimberly and I already had four adopted children but decided that we had room for one more. Our Ukrainian kids also wanted a little brother. After playing with their Ethiopian cousins for a weekend, James said that he wanted a "sunscreen brother!" (He was trying to say "sun-tanned" brother.) So it was a joy to find and adopt Joshua, an adorable five-year-old boy from Ethiopia. His biological parents died when he was one, and he had no siblings. His impoverished uncle put him in an orphanage. Needless to say, we were eager to show him love in many ordinary ways, including family mealtime.

On his second night in our home, we all sat down to eat. Kimberly made a nice meal that included a spinach salad. Our Ukrainian kids never object to vegetables and we had a custom of eating everything on the table. But Joshua wouldn't eat the salad. He wouldn't even eat around the salad. He wouldn't even sit at the table with us! In protest to spinach salad being served, Joshua shook his finger, wagged his head "no," said several Ethiopian words, and left the room! I went to get the little guy, and sat him back at the table. I motioned "eat" with my hands, but it didn't work. He got up two more times to leave the room. I kept bringing him back and sitting him down. He refused to eat spinach.

While this whole episode was going on, I kept thinking about what my mom (and other moms) used to say when I was a kid. She would say, "Tony, you need to eat your green vegetables." I would ask, "Why, Mom?" She would reply something like this: "Because there are starving kids in Africa!" As I surveyed this situation, I thought, *Apparently, that's not true.*

This funny episode actually highlights two basic principles about adoption and orphan care. First, it's *challenging*. Doing orphan care isn't easy. My wife says she never struggled with cussing until she became a mother. Some days I think we will have been successful parents if we keep them out of prison; other days, I think we will have been successful if I stay out of prison.

Second, adoption and orphan care *is a joyful and unpredictable adventure.* Even though you will face challenges, adoption and orphan care will open up emotions you didn't know you had, and you'll have too many stories to share in one lifetime. Despite all the hardships, I wouldn't change our situation one bit. I love being a dad to these five kids. I love seeing Joshua eat his salads now, seeing the kids sing in worship, and seeing them give and receive love.

To endure this joyful but challenging world of orphan care, we need to constantly draw hope and strength from God's Word. *The foundational biblical truths that motivated us to adopt children, sustain us, as well.* Wherever you are in the journey—already adoptive parents, considering adoption, or desiring to do orphan care in other ways— it's important to consider the biblical foundations and the practical challenges carefully.

BIBLICAL FOUNDATIONS FOR ORPHAN CARE

Where should we begin when discussing orphan care? We certainly need to have discussions about adult caregivers/adoptive parents, and orphans, but before we think about people, we need to think about *God*. Let's think about three foundational beliefs about God and the corresponding implications: (1) God cares for everyone made in His image; (2) God is "Father of the fatherless"; (3) God is an adoptive Father.

1. God Cares for Everyone Made in His Image

We get a lot of funny pronunciations of our church name, Imago Dei. One of my friends calls us "Joe Dimaggio Church." One guy said he thought it meant, "I'm a go to church to-dei." Some folks ask us if we are a Hispanic church. Why did we go with this name? My wife and I actually settled on it back in 2005. We said that if we could ever plant a church, we would call it Imago Dei because one of implications of this doctrine is that people have dignity and worth, and we would try to love all types of people. A firm belief in the doctrine of the image of God changes the way we view humanity.

God—who eternally exists in a triune relationship—created the universe out of nothing.[141] The Scriptures speak of God creating "all things,"[142] including the heavens,[143] and His special creation of human beings.[144] The author of Genesis describes God's glorious creation, and says these important words regarding the sixth day:

> Then God said, "Let us make man in our image, after
> our likeness. And let them have dominion over the fish
> of the sea and over the birds of the heavens and over the
> livestock and over all the earth and over every creeping
> thing that creeps on the earth." So God created man in his
> own image, in the image of God he created him; male and
> female he created them.[145]

God delights in His creation, and rejoices in all His works, but He has a unique love for those He made in His own image.[146] Being made in the image of God (or *the imago Dei*) means that people have the capacity to think, feel, reason, love, rejoice, reproduce, choose, and most of all know God personally and eternally through Jesus Christ.[147] God made us intimately, uniquely, and as male and female, distinctly.[148] He also made the purposefully. We are made to glorify the God who made us.

The Psalms are filled with praises to God who created the world in such splendor and glory.[149] Sadly, sin tainted God's glorious creation and is in need of redemption. All of creation, including humans, are under the effects of Genesis 3, and are currently "groaning for redemption."[150] But despite the devastating effects of the fall, we must not take a negative view of creation. We should enjoy creation. We should give thanks to the Creator and Redeemer. And we must assume our responsibility to care for God's creation, giving special attention to God's image bearers. This God-given responsibility involves meeting the physical and spiritual needs of people.

If you don't believe God made and crafted us in His image, then you're left to wonder why you should treat a human with great dignity. But if you embrace the doctrine of the *imago Dei*, you'll care about people from the womb to the tomb. Those who embrace this foundational doctrine will have a different outlook on life than some others. But God's people have always been set apart by such distinction. Pharaoh, Herod, and other evil rulers have had no problems destroying people made in God's image. Many continue to see and treat people as machines, animals, or mere sexual beings. But God's people see things differently. We realize that God's image bearers are worthy of love, dignity, provision, basic rights, and the opportunity to hear the good news about Jesus. In short, we must value what God values, and God values people.

Honoring God, Honoring People

Throughout the Bible, we find that there are no gradations in the image of God. The author of Proverbs tells us:

> The rich and the poor meet together; the LORD is the maker of them all.[151]

> The poor man and the oppressor meet together; the LORD gives light to the eyes of both.[152]

> Whoever mocks the poor insults his Maker; he who is glad at calamity will not go unpunished.[153]

There's no distinction in value here. God made both the rich and the poor, the slave and the oppressor. And notice this: If you dishonor anyone made in God's image, you dishonor God Himself. Similarly, James says:

> But no human being can tame the tongue. It is a restless evil, full of deadly poison. With it we bless our Lord and Father, and with it we curse people who are made in the likeness of God.[154]

Notice the danger of dishonoring those made in God's image by sinning with your words. You must treat humanity with great dignity and care in both word and deed.

Some people don't make this connection between our view of people and our view of God. Consider an illustration from Nicholas Wolterstorff. It would make sense for a foreigner, knowing nothing about U.S. history, to ask, "Why is the Mount Vernon estate in Virginia preserved as a national monument, and treated with great worth?" There are other more elaborate plantation homes. Why is this home so valuable? It's not because of its size or appearance (though it's beautiful). It's significant because it belonged to George

Washington, the first President of the United States. We value the home in Mount Vernon *because we treasure the owner*.[155] Can you imagine the outrage if people were damaging this house? People would speak up and act.

How much more should we care about people made in God's image? Value people because you treasure their Maker. Don't sit idly by while others mistreat God's treasured possession. When we don't act on behalf of God's image bearers, we belittle God Himself.

Martin Luther King Jr. couldn't allow the abuse of *the imago Dei* to go on without acting. This doctrine drove much of the civil rights movement.[156] King fought for fair and just treatment of everyone, and he called out those who discriminated against races. He said:

> You see the founding fathers were really influenced by the Bible. The whole concept of the *imago Dei* . . . is the idea that all men have something within them that God injected. Not that they have substantial unity with God, but that every man has a capacity to have fellowship with God. And this gives him uniqueness. . . . There are no gradations in the image of God. *Every man from a treble white to a bass black is significant on God's keyboard*, precisely *because every man is made in the image of God*. One day we will learn that. We will know one day that God made us to live together as brothers and to respect the dignity and worth of every man. This is why we must fight segregation with all of our non-violent might.[157]

King also reflected on the hypocrisy of a particular white Baptist church that spent thousands of dollars to evangelize Africans, yet fired its pastor for allowing a black man to sing in its choir.[158] His sermons call our attention to the fact that one may affirm the doctrine of *imago Dei* on paper, but actually deny this belief in practice.

Because of a firm belief in the value of everyone, King was moved to tears as he observed the intense poverty in Quitman, Mississippi, specifically as he watched a school teacher feed her students lunch, consisting of only a slice of an apple and some crackers. He grieved over the poor in Harlem, and defended poor sanitation workers in Memphis.

When we ask what drove this great man, we must answer (at least in part): a firm belief in humanity's value and uniqueness. Does it drive you? Do you realize the incredible value of people? C. S. Lewis reminds us of the wonder of a human being:

> There are no ordinary people. You have never talked to a mere mortal. Nations, cultures, arts, civilizations—these are *mortal*, and their life is to ours as the life of a gnat. It is immortals whom we joke with, work with, marry, snub, and exploit.[159]

Because God cares about everyone made in His image, we must too.

2. God Is "Father of the Fatherless"

Some often asked me about this "new orphan-care movement." They wonder about why this movement is growing. The fact is orphan care isn't new. Instagram is new. But orphan care is an old idea.

In the Old and New Testament, we see that God has compassion on the fatherless, and commands His people to mirror His concern. One of God's titles is "Father of the fatherless." It's appropriate in light of the number of texts that highlight God's compassion and care for the orphan. God receives this name like some people receive nicknames—it just reflects His character and nature.

In the Old Testament

As mentioned, the trio of the vulnerable—the orphan, widow, and sojourner—receive special attention in the Old Testament. My friend Rick calls them "running buddies" because you often see them mentioned together. God showed concern for these running buddies, who were vulnerable to abuse and injustice. We could devote an entire chapter to each of these groups of people, but I'm focusing on the orphan here (the others are mentioned throughout the book).

In an effort to highlight the number of texts in a concise way, please notice three charts with three designations: (1) common problems of orphans, (2) God's concern for orphans, and (3) God's commands to care for orphans.

First, consider *some common problems of orphans*. Orphans were some of the most helpless members of society. They were social misfits. They lacked material needs. They were victims of all sorts of abuse. We can piece together a picture of their awful condition by noting a few biblical references.

Common Problems of Orphans	Biblical References
Being Kidnapped and Sold	*There are those who snatch the fatherless child from the breast, and they take a pledge against the poor.* (Job 24:9)
Helplessness	*. . . because I delivered the poor who cried for help, and the fatherless who had none to help him.* (Job 29:12)
Hunger and Abandonment	*If I have withheld anything that the poor desired, or have caused the eyes of the widow to fail, or have eaten my morsel alone, and the fatherless has not eaten of it (for from my youth the fatherless grew up with me as with a father, and from my mother's womb I guided the widow) . . .* (Job 31:16–18)
Losing Land Rights	*Do not move an ancient landmark or enter the fields of the fatherless.* (Prov. 23:10)

Losing Livestock	*They drive away the donkey of the fatherless; they take the widow's ox for a pledge.* (Job 24:3)
Victims of Violence	*You have sent widows away empty, and the arms of the fatherless were crushed.* (Job 22:9)
Treated as Property for which Others Gamble	*You would even cast lots over the fatherless, and bargain over your friend.* (Job 6:27)
Victims of Injustice and Abuse	*Your princes are rebels and companions of thieves. Everyone loves a bribe and runs after gifts. They do not bring justice to the fatherless, and the widow's cause does not come to them.* (Isa. 1:23) *Woe to those who decree iniquitous decrees, and the writers who keep writing oppression, to turn aside the needy from justice and to rob the poor of my people of their right, that widows may be their spoil, and that they may make the fatherless their prey!* (Isa. 10:1–2)
Being Murdered	*They kill the widow and the sojourner, and murder the fatherless.* (Ps. 94:6)
Not Represented in Court	*If I have raised my hand against the fatherless, because I saw my help in the gate, then let my shoulder blade fall from my shoulder, and let my arm be broken from its socket.* (Job 31:21–22)[160]

| Begging for Food and Losing Their Homes | *May his children be fatherless and his wife a widow! May his children wander about and beg, seeking food far from the ruins they inhabit!* (Ps. 109:9–10)[161] |

These same problems continue today. The fatherless are still objects of abuse and exploitation. They often have no one speaking up on their behalf. They are often the poorest of the poor, begging for food, living on the streets, and having serious medical needs. Millions of orphans are around the world right now.

Yet we won't hear them today because they won't make the evening news. Other "more important problems" will get highlighted. You could possibly live your whole life without ever meeting or knowing an orphan. You could live and die and never even be inconvenienced by their presence. You can go about your merry way and never even be moved by their problems because we rarely hear about the orphan crisis. Yet, they're there. Like in the days of the Old Testament, they need advocates, providers, and families.

Second, consider *God's concern for the orphan*. Does anyone care for the vulnerable? Yes. God Himself takes up their concern. The Old Testament writers illustrate God's mercy and compassion with God's concern for orphans.

God's Concern for Orphans	Biblical References
God Hears Their Cry	*If you do mistreat them [orphans and widows], and they cry out to me, I will surely hear their cry.* (Exod. 22:23)

God Defends and Provides for Orphans	*He [God] executes justice for the fatherless and the widow, and loves the sojourner, giving him food and clothing.* (Deut. 10:18)
God Is Entitled "Father of the Fatherless"	*Father of the fatherless and protector of widows is God in his holy habitation. God settles the solitary in a home.* (Ps. 68:5–6a)
God Knows the Orphan's Condition and Will Execute Judgment on Oppressors	*But you do see, for you note mischief and vexation, that you may take it into your hands; to you the helpless commits himself; you have been the helper of the fatherless. . . . you will incline your ear to do justice to the fatherless and the oppressed, so that man who is of the earth may strike terror no more.* (Ps. 10:14, 17b–18)
God Sustains the Orphan	*The LORD watches over the sojourners; he upholds the widow and the fatherless, but the way of the wicked he brings to ruin.* (Ps. 146:9)
God Welcomes the Orphan	*For my father and my mother have forsaken me, but the LORD will take me in.* (Ps. 27:10)
God Shows Mercy to the Orphan	*"Assyria shall not save us; we will not ride on horses; and we will say no more, 'Our God,' to the work of our hands. In you the orphan finds mercy."* (Hos. 14:3)

Third, consider *God's commands to care for orphans*. In light of the plight of orphans, and because of God's concern for orphans, He established laws to help and defend them. We see this plan in the Covenant Code in Exodus, and in the Deuteronomic Code in particular. God had a plan to care for orphans, and that plan was *His people acting justly and mercifully.* God promised to bless those who bless orphans. He warned those who abused orphans. He urged His people to show mercy and justice to them.

God's Commands to Care for Orphans	Biblical References
Don't Take Advantage of Orphans	*You shall not mistreat any widow or fatherless child.* (Exod. 22:22)
Give Justice to Orphans	*"You shall not pervert the justice due to the sojourner or to the fatherless, or take a widow's garment in pledge, but you shall remember that you were a slave in Egypt and the LORD your God redeemed you from there; therefore I command you to do this."* (Deut. 24:17–18)
	"Give justice to the weak and the fatherless; maintain the right of the afflicted and the destitute. Rescue the weak and the needy; deliver them from the hand of the wicked." (Ps. 82:3–4)
	Learn to do good; seek justice, correct oppression; bring justice to the fatherless, plead the widow's cause. (Isa. 1:17)
	"Do not oppress the widow, the fatherless, the sojourner, or the poor, and let none of you devise evil against another in your heart." (Zech. 7:10)

Feed the Orphan from the Third Year's Tithe	*"At the end of every three years you shall bring out all the tithe of your produce in the same year and lay it up within your towns. And the Levite, because he has no portion or inheritance with you, and the sojourner, the fatherless, and the widow, who are within your towns, shall come and eat and be filled, that the LORD your God may bless you in all the work of your hands that you do."* (Deut. 14:28–29)
Provide for the Orphan from the Sheaves Left in the Fields	*"When you reap your harvest in your field and forget a sheaf in the field, you shall not go back to get it. It shall be for the sojourner, the fatherless, and the widow, that the LORD your God may bless you in all the work of your hands."* (Deut. 24:19)
Provide for the Orphan with the Fruit Left on the Trees and Vines	*"When you beat your olive trees, you shall not go over them again. It shall be for the sojourner, the fatherless, and the widow. When you gather the grapes of your vineyard, you shall not strip it afterward. It shall be for the sojourner, the fatherless, and the widow."* (Deut. 24:20–21)

Include Orphans in the Celebrations of the Worshipping Community	*"Then you shall keep the Feast of Weeks to the LORD your God with the tribute of a freewill offering from your hand, which you shall give as the LORD your God blesses you. And you shall rejoice before the LORD your God, you and your son and your daughter, your male servant and your female servant, the Levite who is within your towns, the sojourner, the fatherless, and the widow who are among you, at the place that the LORD your God will choose, to make his name dwell there. You shall remember that you were a slave in Egypt; and you shall be careful to observe these statutes. You shall keep the Feast of Booths seven days, when you have gathered in the produce from your threshing floor and your winepress. You shall rejoice in your feast, you and your son and your daughter, your male servant and your female servant, the Levite, the sojourner, the fatherless, and the widow who are within your towns."* (Deut. 16:10–14)

Know that Condemnation Awaits Those who Oppress Orphans	*"Cursed be anyone who perverts the justice due to the sojourner, the fatherless, and the widow."* (Deut. 27:19)
	"Then I will draw near to you for judgment. I will be a swift witness against the sorcerers, against the adulterers, against those who swear falsely, against those who oppress the hired worker in his wages, the widow and the fatherless, against those who thrust aside the sojourner, and do not fear me, says the LORD of hosts." (Mal. 3:5)

In short, the Old Testament writers reveal why God is called as "Father of the fatherless." He is aware of their awful situation. He is compassionate toward them. He expects and commands His people to care for them.

In the New Testament

Sometimes it's asserted that the New Testament doesn't give much attention to orphan care, and consequently the church shouldn't be all that concerned about it. But I would beg to differ. While the number of texts doesn't compare with the number of Old Testament texts, we must remember that God's character hasn't changed. These Old Testament laws are grounded *in God's character*, which never changes.

Further, the New Testament writers often look back at the Old Testament to base moral and social exhortations for the church. Though the principles for collecting manna don't apply to us, for example, Paul uses them to exhort the church in Corinth to radical generosity and sharing among Christians.[162] Keller notes, "Just as Israel was to be a 'community of justice,' so the church is to reflect these same concerns for the poor."[163]

We see Jesus demonstrating God's ongoing concern for the vulnerable. As noted, Luke describes numerous instances of Jesus caring for the poor. He describes one occasion when a desperate widow from Nain brought her dead son to Jesus. Luke writes that Jesus "had compassion on her" and He then proceeded to raise this young man from the dead. Jesus then gave this boy back to his mother. All the people respond, "God has *visited* his people!"[164] These folks knew that God was "protector of the widow," and that in Jesus, God showed up.

The other Gospel writers also provide examples of Jesus caring for the ostracized, the immoral, children, lepers, and the physically challenged. Matthew and Mark note Jesus' criticism of the religious leaders' insensitivity to the vulnerable, saying they "devour widows' houses and for a pretense make long prayers."[165] And we must remember that the *incarnation* itself was an example of how Jesus "moved in with the poor."[166]

Luke also writes about a very important example of mercy ministry in Acts 6. It's the passage many point to as "the origin of the deacon." The apostles didn't want to give up prayer and ministry of the Word but they had a problem. And what was that problem? It was the need to care for widows. Right here in the beginning stages of the church, the concern for widows appears. Later, when Paul writes to Timothy about the nature of the church, he gives about half a chapter to the proper care for widows.[167]

Though we don't have as many passages on orphan care in the New Testament, we must see the continuity between the Testaments, and consider these New Testament examples. Much of this ministry is assumed. And when you read church history, you find the early church being known for such ministry. The philosopher Aristides told Emperor Hadrian in AD 125 of the early church's praiseworthy mercy ministry, including widow and orphan care: "They love one another, and from widows they do not turn away their esteem; and they deliver the orphan from him who treats him harshly."[168]

The most significant text in the New Testament on orphan care is found in James. Against the backdrop of all the Old Testament texts previously mentioned, James writes these words:

> Religion that is pure and undefiled before God, the Father, is this: to visit orphans and widows in their afflic-tion, and to keep oneself unstained from the world.[169]

James says that faithful Christians care for the vulnerable. And they do it "before God, *the Father*." James seems to intentionally mention the Fatherhood of God in this exhortation. We care for the fatherless in view of, in obedience to, and for the glory of, the "Father of the fatherless." In the context of James, this text serves as a way to be "doers of the word, and not hearers only."[170]

Visiting orphans means to care for them. Know them. Feed them. Teach them. Advocate for them. Welcome them. Give transitional aid to them. Adopt them or, when possible, reunify them. There are vari-ous ways to do James 1:27, but realize it requires personal involvement and sacrifice.

This word *visit* gets used in other very important passages to describe God's merciful care and deliverance of His people in redemptive history.[171] God "visited" His people when they were childless, breadless, and crushed under Egyptian oppression. When God "visited" His people, He came to their rescue personally. James calls us to reflect the nature of our redeeming God by aiding orphans "in their affliction." And the *affliction* exists. Some of the coldest and darkest places I've ever been are orphanages. Not every orphanage cares for children well. In many cases, it's a living hell on earth. Orphans often live in fear, despair, hopelessness, and with the scars of an awful past.

James says caring for orphans in their affliction is one of the marks of "true religion." Yet, how many books on spiritual growth include James's concern? You can find numerous books on Bible study, prayer, stewardship, evangelism, and parenting (and rightly so). But why the neglect of orphan care? Why isn't this on the list of "spiritual disciplines"? Why isn't it known as one of the marks of an effective church? One wonders why James 1:27 isn't taken more seriously, especially given the barrage of the other biblical texts. New Testament scholar Douglas Moo comments on the importance of James 1:27, and the spirit of it:

> One test of pure religion, therefore, is the degree to which
> we extend aid to the "helpless" in our world—whether
> they be widows, orphans, immigrants trying to adjust to
> a new life, impoverished third-world dwellers, the handi-
> capped, or the homeless.[172]

We're left with the question: Am I extending aid to the orphan and other groups of vulnerable people? If not, then why not? God is "Father of the fatherless," and true religion involves imitating His concern.

3. God Is an Adoptive Father

Sometimes people look at me funny when I'm with my Ukrainian son, and my Ethiopian son, since they both call me "Papa." Observers often have questions. As I talk with them, and eventually share that we have five adopted children, the most common question is "Why?"

What moved my heart the most was the doctrine of adoption. Of course, this isn't what most people expect to hear. They expect to hear about infertility. But my wife and I were led to adopt because of *theology* not *biology*.

The doctrine of adoption is the Cinderella doctrine of Pauline theology. Books about salvation often emphasize justification, redemption, reconciliation, and propitiation, but speak cursorily—if at all—about adoption. That's really sad because the doctrine of adoption is, in the words of J. I. Packer, "the highest privilege that the gospel offers."[173]

When we fail to ponder the privileges of adoption, we miss so much. It provides incredible hope and assurance to God's people.[174] It's also a unifying metaphor for much of the Christian life. One can speak of other doctrines when talking about adoption, like the Trinity, salvation, the Spirit, Christian growth, eschatology, the church, and prayer. The doctrine of adoption also inspires prayer and worship to God. And it reminds us of how we should relate to one another in the church: as adopted brothers and sisters.

Paul uses the word *adoption* in Ephesians, Galatians, and Romans, though the concept is taught elsewhere (including in the Old Testament—Israel was "God's son"). Paul shows us that God the Father administered our adoption, God the Son accomplished our adoption, and God the Spirit applied our adoption, giving us a new nature, a new position, and the indwelling presence of God that enables us to cry, "Abba! Father!"[175]

God is an adoptive Father—by choice. Adoption was never Plan B for God. It wasn't an alternative solution. It was Plan A. Before the universe existed, God planned on adopting us into His family.[176] Why did God adopt us? Because He is gracious and merciful. God didn't adopt us because of our attractive merits, but because of His amazing mercy.

Therefore, when Paul tells us to "be imitators of God, as beloved children,"[177] part of that means reflecting the adopting love of God to a world in need. Certainly, not everyone is called to adopt, and not every orphan is available for adoption; but every believer is called to imitate God.

We've passed on "the adoption bug" to our kids. Recently I was taking my son Joshua to baseball practice. He said, "Papa, when I get old, I want to adopt from every country. I want to adopt from Ukraine, Ethiopia, China, and Kentucky." He doesn't understand everything about adoption, but Joshua already has a sensitivity to others in need. His little heart has already grasped the idea that those adopted should extend adopting love to others.

WISE ORPHAN CARE

In light of these foundations, how might we care for those made in God's image? How might we practice true religion? How might we imitate God by putting the adopting love of God on display?

Accept Responsibility

When I talk about orphan care, people usually assume that at the end of the message I'm going to say, "Now, go adopt children!" But that's not my exhortation. I don't tell every Christian to adopt children. I do tell them to elevate their view of adoption, and to seriously consider it. Here's my simple application: Every Christian must *do something* to care for the orphan. The question everyone must ask is, "What can I do to practice James 1:27?" All of us are at various stages of life, and every person needs to pray and evaluate their life before answering this question.

For all of us, orphan care ought to be expressed through very ordinary means. Sure, some of you will be led by the Holy Spirit to pursue international adoptions. Some will rescue multiple siblings in crisis. But others will be called to pursue less costly means in the area of orphan care. While we all are not called to become adoptive parents, we are all called to care for orphans. Orphan care is not for exceptional Christians, it's for the ordinary ones.

One way to love orphans is by caring for *foster children*. Contact your local leaders and see how you can help. Obviously, becoming a foster parent is something every believer should seriously consider. Churches may also think about supporting foster children by providing supplies for them. Some foster children move their stuff from house to house in a garbage bag. Can you imagine a more undignified act? Your church may consider supporting foster children who go to college. Many of them have no parents to move them into a college dorm. They need a computer, a bedspread, a home-cooked meal, and a place to wash clothes and watch football. We shouldn't settle for supply-giving only, but we should see this as a practical way to help and love. You should also consider loving and serving the caseworkers who labor in foster care. Throw them a party as a church and tell them thank you.[178]

Recently, a fifteen-year-old orphan made the news when he attended a worship service in Florida, and asked for someone in the congregation to adopt him. Davion Navar Henry Only, dressed in a dark suit and a borrowed tie, told worshippers at St. Mark Missionary Baptist Church these heart-wrenching words: "I'll take anyone. Old or young, dad or mom, black, white, purple. I don't care. And I would be really appreciative. The best I could be."[179] The fifteen-year-old has been in foster care his whole life. He found out in June that his mother, who gave birth to him while in prison, died.[180] In three years, he'll be on his own. His simple plea was for a family.

I was happy to hear that Davion went to the local church searching for a family. I only wish the local church would start searching for "Davions."

You may also seek to live out James 1:27 by loving the *functionally fatherless*. This generation has been called the *fatherless generation*. We desperately need men in particular to step up and welcome that kid down the street, whose dad is in jail (or uninvolved for other reasons), and whose mom is struggling.

One of my favorite shows growing up was *The Fresh Prince of Bel Air*. Some of you can probably quote the theme song! *It wasn't until recently that I realized I was watching a show about being fatherless.* In an extremely moving episode called "Papa's Got a Brand New Excuse," Will's biological father, Lou, shows up after fourteen years and spends time with him. Will is excited, and comes in with a duffel bag with a gift that's a statue of a father holding his son, saying, "Daddio!" He thinks he's going to go on a trip with his dad. However, his dad lets him down again, making some excuse for postponing the trip. Crushed in despair, but trying to play it off, Will has a conversation with his Uncle Phil. The moving dialogue ends with Will asking Phil, "How come he don't want me, man?"

This pain is present everywhere. And it's not a TV show. Parental abandonment crushes children. Perhaps you won't be an adoptive father, but maybe you can be an Uncle Phil or neighbor that welcomes in the functionally fatherless kid who's asking the question, "How come he [or she] doesn't want me?"

Advocate Boldly

If the Lord gives you any influence, use it to speak up for the voiceless. We've seen in the Old Testament that orphans often had no voice, and God urged His people to treat them justly. The same responsibility falls on us today. In the next chapter, we'll consider the work of advocacy in more detail.

Act Wisely and Holistically

When it comes to *international* orphan care, we must be wise. The orphan crisis is complex, and there isn't just one thing we need to do. If we don't act carefully, we may even end up perpetuating problems (like human trafficking). We also need to think more holistically about orphan care. Adoption is only one of the ways to care for international children. Allow me to list some big categories worth pursuing further. (See Appendix for specific organizations working in these areas.)

Care for the Poor: One of the best ways to care for the orphan is to invest time and resources into impoverished countries, in order to *prevent orphans*. Often, some children are placed into orphanages because of poverty.

Caring for the poor can be a complicated matter, so invest resources, financial and otherwise, wisely. Sometimes we must do emergency relief, but we must also tend to the matters of *restoration* and *development*. Organizations can raise money for emergencies much easier than for development, but if we don't change structures and create sustainability, then the problems may continue to go on. Sometimes we can't prevent children from becoming orphans, but sometimes we can through wise mercy ministry.

One of the ways we need to do this is by mobilizing business leaders to create sustainable businesses in impoverished places. It's common to take a successful businessman or farmer on a mission trip and have him tote bricks for a week. Don't get me wrong; serving is important. But wouldn't it make more sense to tell this same guy to do what he always does: create a sustainable plan for wealth? Wouldn't his entrepreneurial skills serve children and future generations better?[181]

Invest in Orphanages: In many cases, orphans aren't available for adoption. So, the question is, how can we care for kids that will grow up in an orphanage? Perhaps your church can select some orphanages to support. Look to serve orphanages by doing construction work, by giving financial aid, and by supporting the full-time workers. You should also think about how to make sure the children are being taught well, and are learning the basic doctrines of the faith. In supporting orphanages, you may also be able to develop relationships with the children, and have an ongoing relationship with them. Let's do what we can to see that these kids are hearing the gospel, being loved, and are receiving the best possible care.

Promote and Support In-Country Adoption and Orphan Care: While we should commend Americans for adopting a massive number of international children (more than every other country combined),[182] we need to remember that we aren't the only answer to the orphan crisis. If we want to see orphanages emptied, and children in families (where they belong), then we need to think about educating and empowering local leaders to create a culture of adoption and orphan care.

As a political power play in 2012, Vladimir Putin banned American families from adopting Russian orphans. It's infuriating to see orphans used as political pawns, especially when you realize that Americans adopted about 1,000 Russian children in 2011,[183] and that

Americans have adopted more than 60,000 Russian children since the fall of the Soviet Union.[184] But we must also understand that even if the ban didn't exist, there are still nearly 120,000 children in Russia eligible for adoption.[185] What must we do for all these children if we can't possibly adopt them all? We must do our best to train local leaders to care for the orphans in their country. Putin's ban simply illuminates this need.

Since an adoption and orphan-care culture doesn't exist in many countries, we need do what we can to change this. Some of those ways include trying to impact high schools and universities, training pastors and future pastors in seminaries, hosting conferences, writing books, and influencing business leaders and politicians. In some countries, historical myths about orphans abound. Some believe orphans are "cursed," and to bring an orphan in their home is welcoming a curse. So we must educate. Others don't think they have sufficient accommodations to adopt. So we must help provide financial aid.

One agency we support, Lifesong for Orphans, reported recently that they've helped 140 Ukrainian children get adopted by loving, Christian Ukrainian families. They've effectively emptied an entire orphanage. And the cost for a Ukrainian family to adopt a child is $500, not $25,000 (about the cost of an American adopting a Ukrainian).[186] Perhaps you or your church might financially support such initiatives, after doing some careful homework.

Adopt and/or Support Adoption: Adoptions in the United States have decreased significantly in recent years. Will you prayerfully consider adopting children, either domestically or internationally? If the financial challenge is the major obstacle, then consider fostering to adopt. Just remember in adoption to select a good agency, and ask questions.

If you're not able to adopt children, then will you consider supporting others? You might give to various adoption-funding agencies, like our local church does, or you might consider blessing a couple in the adoption process. You may also consider supporting an adoptive couple by helping them tutor their kids, or babysit to give the parents a date night.

Provide Transitional Assistance: Unadopted children often have nowhere to turn when they age out of orphanages. In some international countries, the kids are practically helpless and hopeless. When we were in Ukraine adopting our four children, I remember our driver (who uttered about four words in four weeks) told us when we were finally boarding the train with our kids, "Thank you. These kids have nowhere to go in our country." He wasn't a social worker; he didn't have statistics; but he was savvy. This man knew the underbelly of the country, and he knew that many of the orphans ended up in a life of crime, prostitution, or became victims of human trafficking. His anecdotal statement is verified statistically.

So how do we help? Two ways are obvious. First, *churches must strengthen their relationships with orphanages.* If churches will invest in orphanages, and get to know children, then they can make an impact on these children when they age out. We need to know the kids on a relational level, and seek to support them.

Further, *we must help our Christian businessmen and women get a vision for orphan care.*[187] If entrepreneurial leaders will submit to God's Word, and use their resources, then they can make a huge difference in the lives of children. I would encourage business leaders right now to consider "adopting" an orphanage. They could get to know orphanage leaders now, and provide some immediate help. Then, as the relationship continues, they may begin exploring ways to help these particular kids in the future. What I'm saying is that we need to turn our high capacity leaders loose on this problem of transitional assistance, introducing them to the right people, giving them biblical foundations, and covering them in prayer. We must help and encourage God's people to steward their various gifts and skills for the good of those in need.

Acknowledge Your Insufficiency

Orphan care is warfare. When you begin to minister to orphans you'll face conflict at every level. Don't be surprised when you face challenges within your family and among broken governmental systems. Your marriage may also go through a difficult test as well. All of this and more points to the necessity of prayer. But the good news for Christians is that God is for us. The "Father of the fatherless" is our Abba. The "I AM" who "visited" His people in their affliction in Exodus is with you. Cast your insufficiencies on His total sufficiency. We can cry out to Abba, as Jesus did in the Garden of Gethsemane—weeping and falling to the ground. Because Jesus drank the cup of suffering on our behalf, we aren't orphans any longer. We are children of the Father, and have the ability to seek the Spirit's help, as we minister in Jesus' name.

CHAPTER 4
Courageous Advocacy
How God's People Speak Up for the Voiceless
(with Kimberly Merida)

The purpose of influence is to speak up
for those who have no influence.

RICK WARREN

As we think about the role of advocacy more broadly, I've invited the most influential person to my thinking on these issues to help me write this chapter. My wife Kimberly serves as a volunteer justice advocate for the International Justice Mission, and speaks and blogs about this subject often. We've teamed up to talk about talking.

LAW ENFORCEMENT IS THE INVISIBLE AIR WE BREATHE

We recently moved into a neighborhood behind a high school with no through streets—a perfect place for our kids to ride their bikes. Or so we thought. One afternoon the kids were riding in front of our house while we looked on. Suddenly, a silver car, with squealing tires, fishtailed around the corner and raced past my kids down the street. Thankfully our children quickly hugged the curb to avoid being hit. No sooner had we adults remembered to breathe again, did the car return barreling around the corner with reckless abandon.

I (Kimberly) did what any mama bear would do. I took the license plate down and called the police.

Within five minutes a police officer pulled up to our house just in time for the car to come once again around the corner. Within another few minutes, three more police cruisers arrived with quite a show of force. Children and adults alike looked on with the thrill and in relief of justice being served.

The reality that most poor people live outside the protection of the rule of law is a sobering one.[188] Living in a place where someone will usually answer our call for help provides a subconscious sense of protection. Law enforcement is the invisible air we breathe. We have a voice and a right to protection, even from reckless drivers. We have the right to an attorney, even at no cost if necessary, and all of this is quite empowering.

Imagine not having a voice. Imagine not having an advocate. Imagine not having any law enforcement available to you. No protection. No security.

This is a glimpse into the lives of an estimated four billion poor in the world today.[189]

THE CALL TO SPEAK

God's people have a calling to speak up. I once heard someone share his story of coming to faith and then feeling led to compose a personal mission statement. He then challenged each of us to thoughtfully consider writing our own. I took up this challenge and wrote down what has become my mission statement: I was created to know God and make Him known. This mission helps shape my daily activities. My ability to make God known is contingent upon my knowing the character and mission of our Creator as displayed throughout all of Scripture, particularly in the life and ministry of Jesus. What was Jesus' life and ministry like? Well, hopefully you have already caught on to that from earlier chapters of this book. However, if you haven't, here's the picture: If Jesus, our advocate, was sent to us to proclaim good news and liberty to the poor, captive, and oppressed, aren't we to do likewise?

In the Old Testament, kings were urged to lead the people in defending the weak and the voiceless. In Psalm 72, we find a "royal psalm," which is a prayer for David's line of kings to rule faithfully. The psalm mentions judging righteously, defending the poor, crushing oppressors, delivering the needy when they call, having pity on the weak, and more. This psalm, like Psalm 2, also looks forward to a worldwide rule in which the Messiah will fully execute this vision of peace and justice and righteousness.

When you read the prophets, you find that God rebukes leaders for failing to live out such a dream. Isaiah says, "Learn to do good; seek justice, correct oppression; bring justice to the fatherless, *plead* the widow's cause."[190]

In Proverbs 31, King Lemuel records a charge received from his mother:

> Open your mouth for the mute,
> for the rights of all who are destitute.
> Open your mouth, judge righteously,
> defend the rights of the poor and needy.[191]

Old Testament scholar Duane Garrett comments on this verse, "The plea to 'speak up for those who cannot speak for themselves' is as eloquent a statement of the royal duty of doing justice as one can find anywhere."[192]

Very little information is available about King Lemuel, but the majority of Bible scholars assume he was a king outside of Israel. If this is the case, then this text underscores how all rulers are called to act justly and speak up for the voiceless.

While most of us aren't "kings," one can apply this principle to anyone with influence. If you have a voice, then use it for those who don't—regardless of your position.

The book of Ruth tells the story of a widowed Moabite (Ruth) who meets an Israelite man named Boaz, whom she will eventually marry. Boaz shines as an example of manhood, justice, mercy, and advocacy in a dark period of Israel's history. As Ruth tries to glean in the fields for food, under God's established laws of providing for the poor, she remains dependent on Boaz's favor. Boaz understands that Ruth is vulnerable and in Christlike compassion, he seeks to protect her and preserve her dignity and purity. Boaz tells Ruth not to go into other fields to glean, but to stay with his servants in his field. (Her mother-in-law, Naomi, later warns her about the possibility of being "assaulted" in someone else's field.)[193] Boaz informs Ruth of his protection saying, "Have I not charged the young men not to touch you?"[194]

Boaz does the work of advocacy, speaking on behalf of Ruth, defending and protecting her from harassment and abuse. Professor Daniel Block says, "Contemporary readers will be struck by how modern this comment sounds. Boaz is hereby instituting the first anti-sexual-harassment policy in the workplace recorded in the Bible."[195] Boaz is another example of using one's influence to defend the vulnerable—may his tribe increase!

THE POWER TO SPEAK

Another book of the Bible that has powerful application for advocacy is the book of Exodus. The book opens by explaining Israel's awful slavery, which included four forms of slavery. First, they were under economic/physical slavery, being forced to work "ruthlessly."[196] Second, they experienced political slavery, as powerless refugees living in fear. Third, they were under social slavery, being victims of a state-sponsored genocide. Finally, they experienced spiritual slavery; for the story of Exodus is a story of an ongoing cosmic, spiritual battle. The seed of the serpent, Pharaoh (with the snake headdress), opposes the seed of the woman. But God purposed to redeem them so that they may worship Him[197] and ultimately that all the nations of the world may know His ultimate salvation in Christ.[198] It's hard to worship, or think about anything divine, when you are carrying rocks all day, spending your days in bitter agony. God frees them physically so that they can worship Him spiritually.

From the need for freedom in Exodus 1, we find God's motives for freedom in chapter 2. Consider how God sympathizes with His people's awful condition:

> During those many days the king of Egypt died, and the people of Israel groaned because of their slavery and cried out for help. Their cry for rescue from slavery came up to God. And *God heard* their groaning, and *God remembered* his covenant with Abraham, with Isaac, and with Jacob. *God saw* the people of Israel—and *God knew*.[199]

God heard. God remembered. God saw. God knew. This isn't a distant God, unaware of the cries of the enslaved. He knows the need of the oppressed. And in keeping with His just and merciful character, He will act.

Some evangelicals only apply the book of Exodus to spiritual redemption in Christ. We most certainly should emphasize the greater Exodus accomplished by Jesus, the Greater Moses. And we should beware of some forms of liberation theology that only empha-sizes physical slavery and physical freedom.

But some evangelicals only emphasize the spiritual freedom in Exodus and neglect to note the important socio-political-economic application. I think we should make both applications. God was obvi-ously concerned about both. God cared for the people who were under real physical slavery, and God wanted to bring them out of Egypt for a spiritual purpose. Old Testament theologian Christopher J. H. Wright puts it well:

> Exodus-shaped redemption demands exodus-shaped
> mission. And that means that our commitment to mission
> must demonstrate the same broad totality of concern
> for human need that God demonstrated in what he did
> for Israel. . . . Our mission must be derived from God's
> mission.[200]

In other words, the book of Exodus calls us to imitate God by caring for both physical and spiritual needs of others. We need an integrative model of mission that is biblical and balanced. Let us do evangelism and care for the oppressed.[201]

Some read Exodus and think, *Yeah, God freed Israel from oppression, but that was Israel.* But we must remember why God chose Israel in the first place: to be a blessing to the nations. And God chose them and acted on behalf of them *so that people may know what He is like.* For us, Israel stands as a model as to how God works in the world. In Isaiah 19, even Egypt itself is scheduled for a redemptive blessing when they cry out to the Lord: "When they [Egypt] cry to the LORD because of oppressors, he will send them a savior and defender, and deliver them. . . . the Egyptians will know the LORD in that day and worship . . . and he will listen to their pleas for mercy and heal them."[202] So, Israel stands distinct, but God's liberation of Israel isn't limited to them. Instead, Israel serves as an example of God's mercy and justice for all to see.[203]

GOD LOVES ORDINARY ADVOCATES

An encouraging point to remember about advocacy in Exodus is whom God uses as His spokespersons. God called *Moses* to speak to Pharaoh. Moses made excuses for not wanting to speak, including his lack of credentials, ability to change hearts, and most famously, his lack of eloquence. But the Lord responded to each of these excuses—and to his speech problem—this way:

"Who has made man's mouth? Who makes him mute,
or deaf, or seeing, or blind? Is it not I, the LORD? Now
therefore go, and I will be with your mouth and teach you
what you shall speak."[204]

God said that Moses' lack of communication skills was irreverent and irrelevant. Learn from this. Don't complain about your gifts to your Creator and Redeemer, and don't assume it's all about your ability. It's not. God uses ordinary people to speak up for the voiceless, and He gets all the glory from the victories. Moses learns that even though he is insufficient, God is not. The I AM was with him, and that is all that he needed. God isn't looking for orators; He's looking for obedient speakers who will trust in His sovereign power.

Before Moses' birth, we read of another amazing example of advocacy. In Exodus 1:15–22, we read about the Hebrew midwives. They are honored for their act of preserving life. Interestingly, the name of Pharaoh isn't mentioned, but the midwives names are mentioned: Shiphrah and Puah. These two ladies (who surely had the help of other heroes) serve as examples of justice for us. They fear the real King more than Egypt's king, and don't listen to the decree to kill the innocent.[205] They value human life, and courageously speak and act on behalf of the unborn. They truly live up to their names; Shiphrah means "beautiful one," and Puah means "splendid one." In the midst of wreckage and death, we read of beautiful and splendid acts that led to life, including the birth of Moses, and eventually the birth of Jesus. Without these ladies, we don't have the Exodus, David, Mary, or the Savior. These ladies did something not just for the Hebrews, but for us. Because of their act, under the sovereign hand of God, we believers will rise from the dead. We need an army of people like these ladies, who will speak up for the voiceless in the womb. What a beautiful and splendid thing to do with your life.

THE PRIVILEGE TO SPEAK

In contrast to Israel's captivity in Egypt, those of us who reside in the United States live in a democracy, which brings certain privileges and certain responsibilities. Borrowing from Abraham Lincoln's famous Gettysburg Address, our nation was conceived in liberty and is a government of the people, by the people, and for the people. We have the great privilege of voting and electing representatives to speak on our behalf pertaining to issues we care about. At least that was the idea of our Founding Fathers. These days, however, if you watch the news, it's easy to get disenchanted with the way our system seems to work. In fact, it's easy to get disgusted. My advice? Don't watch it, but don't disengage.

On any given day, there are tens of hundreds of persons descending upon Capitol Hill for the sole purpose of speaking up for various causes. Some are professional lobbyists who represent their clients on important issues like defense appropriations, cancer research funding, school lunches, and renewable energy projects.[206] Others go to lobby for certain peanut oils, equestrian healthcare, and hundreds of other causes. Others take advantages of the right to speak up, and we must embrace this privilege also. And why shouldn't we? Victims of injustice are far more important than peanut oil.

Speaking up for the voiceless is part of ordinary Christian discipleship. It's not all there is to discipleship, but it's part of being salt and light in the world. Take advantage of your privilege to speak, and take responsibility to speak—wisely, compassionately, and prayerfully.

WHY DON'T WE SPEAK?

I (Tony) loved the recent movie about Jackie Robinson entitled 42. In this film, Harrison Ford gives an amazing performance as Branch Rickey, the president and general manager of the Brooklyn Dodgers. He gives us a glimpse of what it looks like to courageously speak up for someone. Rickey brings Robinson to the Dodgers, making Robinson the first African-American player to play in the Major Leagues. Obviously, Robinson has to endure awful mockery and hate-filled criticism, and so does Branch Rickey. In one scene, Rickey shows shortstop Pee Wee Reese a filing cabinet full of hate letters that people have sent to the Dodger president. Rickey does this in order to encourage Reese, who was also receiving criticism for befriending Robinson. Near the end of the movie, Robinson presses Rickey as to why he has submitted himself to the whole painful ordeal. In reply, Rickey tells Robinson of a time that he didn't speak up. When Rickey was in college, the best player on his team was a black man named Charlie Thomas. Sadly, Thomas was ultimately broken by racism. He had no one to speak for him. Rickey then looks at Robinson and says, "There was something unfair about the heart of the game I loved and *I ignored it*. But a time came when I could no longer do that. You let me love baseball again. Thank you."

Have you ever been there? Have you ever known that you should speak up for someone being treated wrongly? If you're like me, you have to admit, like Branch Rickey, we have missed opportunities to advocate for someone.

So why don't we speak up more faithfully—for the racially oppressed, poor, vulnerable, for the orphan, enslaved, for the unborn? Here are some of the main reasons: *ignorance*, *apathy*, and *fear*. Some simply haven't been taught. Others have grown dull and complacent. They have been lulled asleep by the Evil One, living with no sense of urgency. Others stand in fear of man.

But we must add a fourth reason: *despair*. Let me remind you that despair has no place in the life of a Christ-follower, yet we often cave in to this temptation. Responses like heartbreak, grief, and empathy are different from despair. Despair is the complete loss or absence of hope. As sons and daughters of the Most High King, we have hope. We have a calling. We have a privilege. And, there is a great need.

We must put despair to death. See it for what it is. C. S. Lewis writes, "Despair is a greater sin than any of the sins that provoke it."[207] Remember: There's an empty tomb in the Middle East, and an occupied throne in heaven. Remember, your greatest problem has already been solved through the death and resurrection of the now reigning King, who rules over all. You need not be crushed by despair, nor crippled by fear. In the strength that God supplies, speak.

THE NEED TO SPEAK: ORDINARY JUSTICE STORIES

Recently I (Kimberly) was on Capitol Hill to lobby with our representatives on legislation that would strengthen and prioritize the issue of human trafficking. During this time, I met Alex. Our group from North Carolina and those whom we came to meet sat around the table and began to share the reasons why this issue was important to us. Soon it was Alex's turn to tell her story. Pause and read this story about how a five-minute phone call from a caring neighbor saved her life:

> I was adopted at a very young age. The woman who
> adopted me promised my mother to give me a good,
> happy life, but nothing could have been further from
> the truth. I spent the next thirteen years of my life living
> in fear and physical, mental, and emotional torment.
> My adoptive "mother" beat me till my skin was raw,
> threatened to kill me on numerous occasions, and forced
> me to do laborious farm work for an average of eighteen
> hours a day. She gave me caffeine pills to stay awake and
> work into the small hours of the morning. In winter, she
> made me work outside in the cold and dark with no warm
> clothes. If I accidentally fell asleep from sheer exhaustion,
> I was screamed at and beaten and kicked until I mustered
> the strength and energy to go on.

For years, I was trapped in this situation, afraid to leave or to ask anyone for help because I was told that if I ever tried to escape, I would literally be beaten to death. As I was physically assaulted on a near-daily basis, I whole-heartedly believed this threat to be as real and as serious as cancer. Besides this, I was convinced the neighbors would not help were I to go to them anyway. They had seen my sister with a huge black bruise on her eye and done nothing. One neighbor who saw me working in the yard once commented that I should be wearing shoes and I explained honestly that I could not, because it hurt the raw, blistered skin of my feet too much. The neighbor responded with an awkward chuckle and moved along quickly. It was obvious the neighbor had no desire to "get involved in other people's business" but all I could think at the time was how desperately I wanted someone to notice my situation and help me. Eventually, one neighbor had enough. After she witnessed me getting violently slapped in the driveway outside my house, this woman made a call to Social Services and reported the abuse. It's strange to think that a phone call that took about five minutes ended up saving my life; I often wonder how long I would have still been trapped in my hopeless situation had that neighbor decided not to act. I am forever grateful for that woman's boldness to step in and care about a situation that had nothing to do with her, because it meant everything to me. Because of her, I now know freedom. I now have the passion, and the ability, to help others the way I once was helped. Now, I am free and will do anything in my power to be an advocate for those who are voiceless and oppressed.

When Alex finished sharing a piece of her story there was a deep sense of personal affirmation in the cause, to speak up and defend the rights of the poor and oppressed.

This example of neighbor love was quite compelling. Alex's passion to help others by speaking up infuses great hope for the rescue and restoration of others in similar situations.

This next story continues to weigh heavy on me, making the task of retelling quite an arduous one. This is a story of a young friend named Mia.[208] I (Kimberly) met her shortly after celebrating her sixteenth birthday. She had transferred from an aftercare ministry on the other side of the state to one that was close by, having been in the "system" since age fourteen. In the year that followed, we visited together on numerous occasions including a few weekends at our home as a means of respite care for the shelter staff. One afternoon after sharing a meal together, she began to expose some of the darkness that has claimed her past. Below is my attempt to grant you a glimpse into her reality.

When Mia was twelve years old, everything she thought she knew about the world and whatever safety she had previously felt began to crumble. She not only endured the physical trauma of being raped, but the psychological devastation of the loss of trust or reliability of another. You see, the perpetrator was her very own father. As you can imagine, this traumatic experience sent Mia spiraling in a grievous state of loss and turmoil. This loss of trust created a feeling of being unsafe and without protection. Her perceived place of security was void.

Those who were to protect Mia, and speak up for her, were silent. When the trauma occurred, as it did for Mia, in early adolescence, it disturbed the formation of a healthy development of identity, resulting in a loss of self and helplessness.[209] In her distress, she sought a new protector and provider. This search led her to the arms of one she thought to be her boyfriend. Following a process of luring (playing the role of boyfriend, protector and provider of nice things) and grooming (providing drugs and intimacy), he began pimping her out to others in his gang, as well as to anyone willing to pay for her services. Mia despairingly found herself the victim of sex trafficking.

The abuse Mia endured from her earthly father and other men has become a stumbling block to comprehending and embracing the love of her heavenly Father—the One who will "maintain the cause of the afflicted and execute justice for the needy."[210] Though she has been physically liberated from the bondage of sexual enslavement and has had the gospel of Jesus Christ shown and spoken to her, she still struggles to grasp God's redemptive love for her. This continues to grieve me, particularly when I receive text messages from her now reintegrated into normal life that demonstrates her continued pursuit of comfort and security in temporal arenas. I rest in the reality that Christ is our hope. Christ alone can take victims of injustice who have lost innocence, lost trust, lost their identity, and bind up all their broken pieces.

Mia showed me a scar from a tattoo that had been removed from her wrist. It had been a means of branding in order to show ownership by the gang who had previously enslaved her. She looked at me through unshed tears and shared how she wanted one day to get a new tattoo to cover those scars. One for each wrist that displayed the words *hope* and *redeemed*. (She loved Francine Rivers's historical fiction account of Hosea and Gomer in her book called *Redeeming Love*.) I shared with her that my prayer was and continues to be that Christ our Savior would tattoo those words on her heart and soul. That she would come to a saving and liberating knowledge of the Redeemer who loves her with an unending, never giving up, always and forever kind of love.

Mia's story is tragically reminiscent of many before her and many today. Recall the story of Tamar in 2 Samuel 13:1–22, who was raped by her half-brother, Amnon. She is then told to keep silent by another brother, Absalom. She also witnesses her father, King David, despite being angry, do nothing to punish the guilty. As a women's teacher and nurse for two decades, Barbara Smith describes the ramifications experienced from this atrocity, "No one spoke life or hope to her; in other words, her hopelessness led to depression as she became a woman without a voice."[211]

Consider a few stories encountered through the work of justice ministries abroad. Ponder Grace's story, a lady from Zambia. When her husband passed away in 2008, Grace suddenly came under threat from relatives who wanted control of her home. Her stepchildren bullied her constantly, stole her belongings, and even threatened to kill her. She lived in fear that they would attack at any moment. She tried to resolve the situation on her own, but after a while, one stepson brazenly seized the house and cut off Grace's only source of income. The International Justice Mission in Zambia protected Grace and gave her the support she needed. IJM attorneys defended Grace's rights in court and stood up against her abusive stepchildren in a tense six-month trial. Thankfully, in July 2013 the Zambian judge ruled in her favor, granting her home back. You can read more stories like this on IJM's website: www.ijm.org/news.

Consider the story of James Kofi Annan who lives in Ghana. Once a child slave himself, he now works to rescue children caught in the slave trade and provide opportunities for these children to receive an education. In Ghana, parents unknowingly and knowingly sell their children into slavery to fishermen in order to wrangle their fishing nets for up to seventeen hours a day. Joshua is one of the children Annan has saved from slavery. He has scars where he was hit depending on his so-called mistakes. Scars on the side of his body, because he could not dive as deep as twenty meters, and on the head, for throwing nets the wrong way.[212] Seeking to establish laws to protect children, as well as by providing education opportunities for victims rescued from slavery, is how Annan speaks up for the oppressed in his land. You can read this story and more stories like this on CNN's Freedom Project web page.

There are countless other stories that could be told here from every corner of the world, including our own backyard. The need is great. But our God is greater. So, for all the Alex's, Mia's, Tamar's, Grace's, James' and Joshua's out there, let us rise up to the task of displaying through word and deed the character of our God, who is the *Father of the fatherless* and *protector of widows*.[213] Will you speak up for them?

WAYS TO SPEAK

Speaking up, if you recall Proverbs 31:8–9, starts with opening your mouth. This begins by simply living sensitively to the needs around you, and around the world. When you sense injustice, speak up about it, as illustrated in the story of Alex and her caring neighbor who called Social Services.

To live a sensitive life, seek God through Scripture and prayer daily. Remember the lessons from Wilberforce's walk with God, and follow this pattern of daily communion with God. You may also consider hosting a Bible study to delve deeper into God's heart of justice displayed throughout the Scriptures.[214]

Another way to use your voice for the voiceless is in the context of lobbying our governing leaders. As mentioned, lobbying is simply asking an elected or appointed official to take a particular position, or to vote in a particular way on a specific piece of legislation. When you lobby, you are serving as a bridge between your elected government official and the people in your community.[215] In other words, when you lobby you stand in the gap between your neighbors and your leaders. You can exercise this great privilege by contacting local and state leaders.

Speaking up to our governing authorities is a multilayered task. This requires people to mobilize at all levels in order to engage an effective, comprehensive approach to combating issues of injustice. This can be as simple as making phone calls, writing letters, or signing online petitions to your representatives. It's important to note, however, that the most effective tool in lobbying is to make a personal visit to your representatives. The International Justice Mission has released a tool specifically designed to equip you further on how to speak truth to power called *The Advocate's Handbook: A Blueprint for Building Your Advocacy Campaign.*

Additionally, you might consider creative ways to steward your various areas of influence. Plan an event. Invite your coworkers and friends. Use the opportunity to share stories of injustice. Be sure to share tangible ways they can get involved. If we simply end the story with the burden of the problem, the temptation of despair can creep in. Provide practical action steps through your event for people to be more than hearers but doers. Some examples of events to consider range anywhere from sharing with your mothers' day out group, coffee with friends or business associates, hosting a house concert, planning a town hall event, presenting a paper for your class, screening a documentary at your social organization, or hosting a church-wide gathering centered on the issue of injustice.

Consider writing a blog to your readers or encouraging someone else who blogs to highlight a particular issue of injustice. Post a Facebook comment or tweet weekly with links to various justice-seeking ministries and organizations. Write an op-ed for your local news source. In these examples, be sure to do some research, utilize credible information, and provide additional resources for further study. Be aware of the fact that it is easy, as well as dangerous, to speak with a false sense of authority, make sweeping generalizations, or perhaps even disclose information that can re-victimize or increase vulnerabilities for the very ones you seek to speak up for.

A personal example of this involves a time I had visited a vulnerable community in Southeast Asia where sex trafficking was rampant. Chronicling my experiences through a blog for friends back home, I shared the realities of this heinous injustice and disclosed the name of each place I had been. Thankfully, a friend from IJM saw my post and graciously provided helpful instruction of how to educate others while protecting the vulnerable in the process. Despite the prevalence of sex trafficking in this community and previous media attention this location had received, there are still countless predators who surf the Internet regularly in a scenario that looks a lot like Psalm 10:8–9 depicts.

> He sits in ambush in the villages;
>> in hiding places he murders the innocent.
> His eyes stealthily watch for the helpless;
>> he lurks in ambush like a lion in his thicket;
> he lurks that he may seize the poor;
>> he seizes the poor when he draws him into his net.

Be wise in your speaking up.

Brothers, this last example of speaking up is particularly directed to you. The outrageous, incestuous rape of Tamar back in 2 Samuel 13 actually began when his friend Jonadab provided Amnon with a serpent-like scheme to lure her to Amnon's bedroom. This is an example of a brother encouraging the preying on of younger women. Brothers, do not engage in corrupt talk, crude joking, and deceitful desires. Instead, have the integrity to speak against sexual assault, pray for your sisters, and take on the role of protector. Can you hear Tamar's cries to her brothers? "Speak up for me!" Can you hear Mia's cries? "Speak up for me!" Can you hear the countless other voices crying out from their oppression? "Speak up for me!"

The brothers of the Shulamite in Song of Solomon provide a vivid portrait of what godly men should look like.[216] The brothers were to surround their young sister to protect her purity. Some prey and devour young ladies, but true brothers will protect their sisters.[217] Which are you: predator or protector?

For the Christian, we should know and appreciate advocacy. For Christ is our Great Advocate![218] Jesus is the one who has acted righteously, and now stands in the presence of our Father to speak on behalf of those who haven't acted righteously.[219] Because we stand accepted before God, through the cross-work and intercession of Jesus, we can speak courageously. Because of Christ, we need not fear death or people. And the Spirit now empowers us to speak the truth in love. So let us advocate for others, as servants of the Great Advocate, for the good of the voiceless.

Sure, there is a sense in which Washington, City Hall, and your neighborhood association change policies based on insider political techniques. But God's call to advocate for others is not a call to develop tradecraft as a professional lobbyist—though if you do, more power to you! The call to ordinary advocacy is to imitate your Advocate by speaking up wherever He has placed you in life. Who knows? Maybe if we all speak up, something extraordinary will happen.

CHAPTER 5
God-Centered Humility
How an Ordinary Christian Walked with His Extraordinary God

Almighty God, who created us in your image:
Grant us grace fearlessly to contend against evil
and to make no peace with oppression; and, that we may
reverently use our freedom, help us to employ it in the
maintenance of justice in our communities and among
the nations, to the glory of your holy Name; through Jesus
Christ our Lord, who lives and reigns with you and the
Holy Spirit, one God, now and for ever. Amen.

THE BOOK OF COMMON PRAYER

William Wilberforce was an ordinary Christian. A mere five feet three, Wilberforce's chest only measured thirty-three inches. Once, his weight dropped to seventy-six pounds when he had an illness. If you met him today, you'd find it hard to believe that he could amount to much.

Yet, Os Guinness calls him "the most successful social reformer in the history of the world."[220] In Eric Metaxas's wonderful book *Amazing Grace: William Wilberforce and the Heroic Campaign to End Slavery*, he rightly says, "If ever someone could restore our ability to again see simple goodness, it should be Wilberforce."[221] Because of this, he's worthy of our consideration and emulation. You don't have to be physically impressive to change the world. You simply need to know what Wilberforce knew; Eric Metaxas tells us:

> Great men like Wilberforce and Wesley had the humility and wisdom to know that whatever strengths they had— and they had many—they could not win without total reliance on God. . . . These men were able to succeed only because they humbled themselves and entrusted the battle to God.[222]

What made him great? Answer: God-centered humility.

ORDINARY FOR THE SAKE OF OTHERS

Wilberforce fought against slave trade and slavery itself for almost *forty-six years*! At age twenty-five he was converted, and then considered leaving Parliament for vocational ministry. Fortunately for the rest of the world, John Newton talked him out of it, urging him to fight injustice through politics. Wilberforce eventually surrendered to this noble calling, saying, "God Almighty has set before me two Great Objects: the suppression of the Slave Trade and the Reformation of Manners."[223] By the "reformation of manners" he meant attacking other social problems of his day, including child labor and sex trafficking.[224] At one point, he was linked with sixty-nine separate groups dedicated to social reform.[225]

Wilberforce demonstrated remarkable humility when he gave up the chance to be prime minister of England "for a cause that to him was far greater than becoming the leader of the greatest empire in the world at that time."[226] Metaxas writes:

> He gave up his life for the sake of African slaves, people who could give him nothing in return. But Wilberforce knew that what God had given up for him was far greater,

so he did what he did for the Africans he would never meet, and for God.[227]

Notice the nature of justice work. It's often done without receiving any reward in this life. Those you serve may never thank you. And you may have to give up opportunities and positions in order to do it. But the sacrifice is worth it when you value people, and desire the glory of God above all things.

After working for twenty years to abolish the slave trade, Wilberforce fought another twenty-six years to abolish slavery itself. And it, too, was eventually abolished just three months before he died.

TWO TYPES OF MEN

While men today work religiously at gyms, and look impressive on the outside, our generation lacks a Wilberforce. The world needs contemporary examples of men who defend the weak. Where is he?

Men are often *abusive* or *passive*. Both of these problems are products of living in a fallen world. When sin entered the world, God told Adam that he would be tempted to either dominate or be passive.[228] As a result, men are often known for being *bullies* or *cowards*.

Look at television shows today. How are men most often portrayed? Rarely do we find the strong defending the weak. John Wayne remains popular, in part, because in his films he took up for the powerless. So did Chuck Conners in *The Rifleman*. I remember watching *The Rifleman* with my dad as a boy. I loved that show, and it had a constant message to young boys: Don't be a bully or a coward.[229]

Injustice exists because men either abuse the weak or fail to defend the weak. We need a revival of honorable men, men who are both tough and tender. How can we create such a culture? How might we cultivate hearts of humility and sacrifice—characteristics of Jesus?

Internet pornography, excessive video gaming, and the overall feminization of men will never produce the kind of men who passionately and constantly do Micah 6:8. We need another method. We need to ask, "What made Wilberforce different? How was humility and sacrifice cultivated in his heart?" Let me point out four ingredients of his greatness.

Conversion, Scripture, Prayer, and the Glory of God

Conversion: Wilberforce didn't simply decide to start doing good things. Everything changed when he was converted at age twenty-five.[230] In fact, he called his conversion "The Great Change."[231] He had several objections to Christianity but was eventually won over. Isaac Milner, a prestigious professor at Cambridge, was particularly influential in leading Wilberforce to Christ.[232]

Metaxas says that the most obvious sign of his conversion was that it changed the way he looked at the rest of the world. He writes:

> Suddenly, he saw what he was blind to before: that God was a God of justice and righteousness who would judge us for the way we treated others; that every single human being was made in God's image and therefore worthy of profound respect and kindness; that God was "no respecter of persons" and looked upon the rich and poor equally. . . . For the first time in his life, Wilberforce saw the world through God's eyes.[233]

Wilberforce's courageous agenda stemmed from his new affections and this new vision of the world. Chuck Colson wrote that Wilberforce's conversion led him to the belief that, "If Christianity was true and meaningful, it must not only save but serve. It must bring God's compassion to the oppressed as well as oppose the oppressors."[234] He also believed that a heart change was the ultimate hope for others.

John Piper notes, "He believed with all his heart that new affections for God were the key to new morals and lasting political reformation."[235]

While we don't have the same calling as Wilberforce (namely, to serve the oppressed through politics), we can know the same Savior Wilberforce knew. We can, in the words of the apostle Paul, become "a new creation" in Christ Jesus.[236] Has that happened to you?

Perhaps you wonder, "Can't we just do justice, and leave out all this talk about conversion?"

Sure, a person may do good in this world, since he or she bears the image of God. Human beings solve many problems, and we should gladly work alongside nonbelievers when it is wise to do so. So why emphasize conversion?

First, apart from conversion, a person will have different motives for service, and motives matter to God. Why are you doing mercy and justice? This is a very important question. Second, a Christian pursues justice with an amazing sense of hope and power. They realize that the Spirit is empowering them, and that the glory of God will soon cover the earth as the waters cover the sea—and these truths provide amazing hope and power for doing justice.[237] Third, unbelievers must realize that no amount of social justice can merit eternal life. Learn from Wilberforce. You and I need Jesus. We need Him for us to be saved from His just judgment. We need Him for us to see the world correctly. We need Him for sustaining power and hope as we labor in this broken world.

Scripture: The gospel that brought Wilberforce to faith in Christ was the same gospel that he meditated on constantly. He loved "the peculiar doctrines" of the Christian faith contained in Holy Scripture. This phrase referred to the doctrines like "human depravity, divine judgment, the substitutionary work of Christ on the cross, justification by faith alone, regeneration by the Holy Spirit, and the practical necessity of fruit in a life devoted to good deeds."[238] He believed that the moral decay of his time was the result of losing sight of such doctrines.[239]

Wilberforce saw these doctrines as central, not only for the good of individuals' salvation, but also for the good of culture. He stated,

"The grand radical defect in the practical system of these nominal Christians, is their forgetfulness of all the peculiar doctrines of the Religion which they profess—the corruption of human nature—the atonement of the Savior—the sanctifying influence of the Holy Spirit."[240]

Consider an example of how meditating on the gospel changes lives and cultures. Let's return to the problems of *abuse* and *passivity*. The good news of the gospel is that a person is made both *humble and courageous* at the same time. You can be courageous because Christ has taken care of your greatest fears; namely, death and judgment. Because of this, we don't need to fear rejection from others, seek approval from others, or even fear death. We're free to live courageous lives, saying like Paul, "To live is Christ, and to die is gain."[241] The gospel also creates humility: we know we've done nothing to deserve redeeming grace. We can identity with the weak and the powerless, for we were weak and powerless before Christ rescued us. We will gladly take up for the enslaved, the orphaned, and the abused because there's a real sense in which we see ourselves there. We can associate with the lowly because we understand and sympathize with them. Gospel-centered people should be the most courageous and humble people on the planet.

Wilberforce meditated on the peculiar gospel doctrines revealed in Holy Scripture on a regular basis. He loved the Scripture so much that he memorized passages, including Psalm 119, which has 176 verses! He would sometimes walk two and a half miles from Parliament to his house. The last part of the walk took him through Hyde Park, which is where he would often recite this long psalm. (Psalm 119 is about the importance of God's Word shaping one's life and thoughts.) Wilberforce knew that if he started reciting it when he entered the park, then he would finish (in twenty minutes) when he got home.[242] Picture this extremely busy man reciting Psalm 119 walking through the park. See the relationship between meditating on Scripture and changing the world through courageous justice work.

Metaxas summarizes, "William Wilberforce was someone who took the Bible seriously, and as a result of this belief, he literally changed the world."[243]

Prayer: Wilberforce demonstrated humility through his personal and communal prayer life. He prayed by himself, he prayed with others, and he had others praying for him.

Wilberforce's friend John Wesley once wrote him a letter encouraging him to labor on. It may have been the last letter ever written by the eighty-seven-year-old Wesley. He told Wilberforce:

> Unless God has raised you up for this very thing, you will
> be worn out by the opposition of men and devils. But if
> God be for you, who can be against you? O be not weary
> of well doing. Go on, in the name of God and in the
> power of his might, till even American slavery (the vilest
> that ever saw the sun) shall vanish away before it.[244]

Notice that even the best of men need encouragement and the prayers of others. Wilberforce didn't do his work as an isolated individual. He benefited from Christian community, in particular the community known as "Clapham Circle." Wilberforce's friend, John Thornton, purchased a big house in order to cultivate community. In the mornings, people would gather for breakfast and prayer, and whenever an important bill was being passed, it would become a matter of prayer.[245]

We learn from Wilberforce the importance of doing mercy and justice in community, and with a deep devotion to prayer. Justice and mercy ministry advocates will face spiritual warfare, and must pray for and with one another, and constantly encourage each other.

The Glory of God: Wilberforce viewed his work from a God-centered perspective, not merely from a political perspective. John Piper says:

He was not a political pragmatist. He was a radically
God-centered Christian who was a politician. And his true
affections for God based on the *"peculiar doctrines"* of
Christianity were the roots of his endurance for in the
cause of justice.[246]

Another biographer wrote of his motives, saying:

The primary driving force behind Wilberforce's legislative
perseverance was not, like most politicians before and
since, to pass laws that would bring benefits to society;
it was to pass laws to eradicate the activities that were
offensive to God. . . . William Wilberforce's secret was that
he made the journey from self-centeredness, achievement-
centeredness, and political-centeredness to *God-
centeredness*. And he made it with *Christlike joy*.[247]

Oh, for more Wilberforces! Will you consider pouring out your
life for the good of others and the glory of God with Christlike joy?

Will You Meditate on God's Word?

It's essential to meditate on God's Word, because we behold the
glory of God in His Word. This is critical because *we become like that
which we worship*. This fact is evidenced all around us, but it's also a
common theme in the Bible.[248] Personal heart transformation doesn't
happen simply by information transfer. It happens as you adore God,
based on His revelation of Himself in the Word. If we can behold
Him, admire Him, esteem Him, enjoy Him, and be captivated by
Him, then we will imitate Him.

Let's stop and meditate on God's Word right now for a moment.
Consider Psalm 146. The legendary preacher Charles Spurgeon was
known for his incredible preaching ability, but he also had a tremen-
dous heart for and ministry to the poor, the widow, and the orphan.
He once preached a sermon entitled, "The Lord's Famous Titles"

on Psalm 146:7–9. The psalm speaks of who God is. How might you introduce God? Pause and read this slowly, paying particular attention to verses 7–9.

> [146:1] Praise the Lord!
>   Praise the Lord, O my soul!
>   [2] I will praise the Lord as long as I live;
>   I will sing praises to my God while I have my being.
>   [3] Put not your trust in princes,
>   in a son of man, in whom there is no salvation.
>   [4] When his breath departs, he returns to the earth;
>   on that very day his plans perish.
>   [5] Blessed is he whose help is the God of Jacob,
>   whose hope is in the Lord his God,
>   [6] who made heaven and earth,
>   the sea, and all that is in them,
> who keeps faith forever;
>   [7] *who executes justice for the oppressed,*
>   *who gives food to the hungry.*
> *The Lord sets the prisoners free;*
>   [8] *the Lord opens the eyes of the blind.*
> *The Lord lifts up those who are bowed down;*
>   *the Lord loves the righteous.*
>   [9] *The Lord watches over the sojourners;*
>   *he upholds the widow and the fatherless,*
>   *but the way of the wicked he brings to ruin.*
>   [10] The Lord will reign forever,
>   your God, O Zion, to all generations.
> Praise the Lord! (my emphasis)

The psalmist desires a life of sustained praise. This is essential because we minister out of the health of our soul (vv. 1–2). We need to daily have our affections stirred, and serve out of the overflow of a heart in awe of God. The psalmist also tells us to trust in God, not man (vv. 3–4). Then he proceeds to tell us about why God is worthy of worship and trust in the following verses. Spurgeon pointed out that God is "The Emancipator," who frees the spiritual prisoner. He is "The Illuminator," who opens the eyes of the spiritually blind. God is "The Comforter," who lifts up the burdened and bereaved. He is "The Rewarder," who loves the righteous. And God is "The Preserver," who preserves the strangers, relieves the widow and fatherless, and executes justice on the wicked.[249]

Is this the vision of God that most people have? How would people today introduce God? Perhaps phrases like this: "He is a distant creator, who created the world but is uninvolved in it," or "All religions believe in the same God," or "God wants people to be nice, good, and feel good about themselves; and when they die, He will take everyone to heaven."

The good news is God has not left us in the dark about who He is. The person trying to describe God apart from the Bible is like the person trying to introduce a speaker that they know nothing about. Imagine if someone introduced me at an event saying, "Tony is here to speak today. He likes country music, cats, and NASCAR." None of that is true. Not even close. But that's what people do when they try to explain God apart from His Word. Thankfully, God has told us what He's like in Scripture. Don't believe in the god of your imagination. Believe in the God of biblical revelation.

If you will accept God as He's presented in His Word, then you will discover a gloriously attractive God who saves sinners and takes up the cause for the powerless. Tim Keller puts it like this:

> When people ask me, "How do you want to be introduced?" I usually propose they say, "This is Tim Keller, minister of the Redeemer Presbyterian Church in New York City." Of course, I am many other things, but that is the main thing I spend my time doing in public life. Realize, then, how significant it is that the biblical writers

introduce God as a "father to the fatherless, a defender of widows" (Psalm 68:4–5). This is one of the main things he does in the world. He identifies with the powerless, he takes up their cause.[250]

When you marvel at the nature of God, you'll begin to imitate Him before a broken world. This is the true starting place for a life of justice and mercy. In her book *Deepening the Soul for Justice*, Bethany Hoang says it well, "Seeking justice doesn't begin at the door of a brothel. Seeking justice begins with seeking the God of justice."[251] See and savor the God of the Bible, and allow that vision to transform your heart like it did for Wilberforce.

Part of our problem with reading the Bible is our cultural presuppositions. What if you were the victim of constant and terrible injustice, and the first Bible story you ever read was Naboth's Vineyard? How might your view of God be formed then?

This actually happened. Chris Wright tells the story about a young man from India who read the Bible for the first time. For whatever reason, the first passage he read was this uncommon story about Naboth. Wright was teaching at a conference from the Old Testament when he met this young man. The young man told Wright that he became a Christian through his journey in the Old Testament, and he was particularly thrilled that they would be studying the Old Testament in the sessions. Wright tells how this young reader was drawn to the God in the story of Naboth's Vineyard:

> He grew up in one of the many backward and oppressed groups in India, part of a community that is systematically exploited and treated with contempt, injustice, and some-times violence. The effect on his youth was to fill him with a burning desire to rise above that station in order to be able to turn the tables on those who oppressed him and his community. . . . He was contacted in his early days at college by some Christian students and given a Bible,

which he decided to read out of casual interest, though he had no respect at first for Christians at all.

It happened that the first thing he read in the Bible was the story of Naboth, Ahab, and Jezebel in 1 Kings 21. He was astonished to find that it was all about greed for land, abuse of power, corruption of the courts, and violence against the poor—things that he himself was all too familiar with. But even more amazing was the fact that God took Naboth's side and not only accused Ahab and Jezebel of their wrongdoing but also took vengeance upon them. Here was a God of real justice. A God who identified the real villains and who took real action against them. "I never knew such a God existed!" he exclaimed. He read on through the rest of OT history and found his first impression confirmed. . . .

He then went on, he told me, to read the books of the law, and his amazement grew. "God!" he cried out, even though he didn't know who he was talking to, "You're so perfect! You think of everything!" . . . He found himself praising this God he didn't know. "God, you're so just, you're so perfect, you're so holy!" he would exclaim, believing this was the kind of God that answered the need of his own angry struggle.

Then he came upon Isaiah 43:1, and came to an abrupt halt. "But now, says the Lord . . ." It's a beautiful word in Telugu, apparently. It means, "yet, in spite of all that." The end of Isaiah 42 describes Israel's sin and God's just punishment. But suddenly, unexpectedly, God is talking about forgiveness and pardon and love. "I couldn't take that," he said. "I was attracted to the God of justice and holiness. I ran away from a God of love." But he couldn't. For as he read on he found such a God more and more—still in the OT! It was about then that the

Christian friends came and explained more about the full-ness of God's justice and love on the cross, and he came at last to understand and surrender to the God he had found in the OT and his life was transformed through faith in Christ. . . .

"I never knew such a God existed." But he does—not just in the past of ancient Israel, but in today's world. Are we afraid to discover him?[252]

I love that response: "I never knew such a God existed." Do you know this God exists? Do you know how He is presented in the Word? Do you know that He welcomes you into a relationship with Him, through Jesus Christ? Do you know that He calls you to imitate Him? He does, my friend. The question is: "Does this move you?" like it moved this young man in India? Let me encourage you to seek God daily in His Word that you may know Him truly, and make Him known practically.

To do the work of justice, we must be humble and teachable. We must mediate on God's Word, and we must never stop learning God's Word (and ways to fight for justice). Never think you've arrived. Humble yourself as a learner.

Will You Seek God in Prayer?

We'll never cultivate humility apart from dependent prayer. Prayerlessness clearly demonstrates a belief in our own self-suffi-ciency. When I'm not praying, and sadly this is too often, I'm basi-cally saying, "I've got this. I don't need God's help." In doing this, I'm insulting God, and accomplishing nothing. Courageous humil-ity flows from powerful communion with God, as illustrated by Wilberforce and his friends.

Each year the International Justice Mission's Global Prayer Gathering assembles in the D.C. area for the purpose of seeking God in desperate prayer. My wife has attended numerous times, and I have had the joy of being there twice. The first time I attended, I didn't really know what to expect. Do people actually show up just to pray? After some moving worship and fellowship on the opening night, Saturday proved to be a life-changing experience for me.

We went in one room after another, hearing updates from the field. After hearing reports we prayed. We prayed for victim relief, victim aftercare, perpetrator accountability, and spiritual and structural transformation.

IJM calls their Saturday prayer time, "Doing the work of justice." It's properly named because it's labor. Often times, we think about prayer as preparation for the work, when in reality, it's the work. It's not all we do, but it's central to it. Justice people should be *praying people*.

We poured out our hearts for young girls who were being drugged and raped multiple times a day. We cried out for widows who were having their land taken from them by violent oppressors. We celebrated victories of perpetrators being held accountable, and we prayed for more cases of just prosecution. After hearing each story, I was made aware of how intense this matter of justice ministry really is. The battle is fierce, and raging, but God's people have a prayer-answering God. We can cry out to Him on behalf of the oppressed.

When the day was over, I remembered what Paul said about Epaphras. He said, "Epaphras, who is one of you and a servant of Christ Jesus, sends greetings. He is always *wrestling in prayer* for you."[253] Wrestling leaves you exhausted. And real intercessory prayer will take time and energy too. When was the last time you were exhausted after pouring out your heart to God on behalf of others?

While I certainly want to encourage an "as you go" prayer life, I want to also encourage you to spend unhurried and unhindered times in focused prayer. We must not relegate our prayer life to multitasking. Jesus Himself had times in which He got alone to pray.[254]

IJM also taught me about this too. I read where, upon entering the office, they turn off everything and spend thirty minutes with

God, making a declaration "that the first work of justice is the work of prayer."[255] But that's not all. They do it again at 11 a.m.—only this time, all together.

Our pastors and wives made a visit to their offices last year and they invited us to their 11 a.m. prayer time. Every IJM office around the world shares in this practice, at their own appointed time. They come together, read Scripture, and listen to prayer requests related to their work of justice going on around the world. Then they intercede on behalf of these needs. Our elders heard stories, and the hearts of these laborers, and we joined them in prayer.

Don't miss this picture; these are professional leaders, dressed in formal business attire, literally changing the world everyday. Yet, each individual stops before they type a sentence or make a phone call for thirty minutes of personal prayer. Then, they assemble together at 11 a.m. for corporate prayer. These are busy people. But their theology tells them that prayer isn't ceasing from the work of justice; it's an essential part of the work of justice.

Their focus on prayer reminded me of the early church in Acts 4. When they were persecuted, they prayed to God, asking for boldness in their witness.[256] They didn't pray for escape from the situation, but for courage. And God answered their prayer.

Let me encourage you to find practical ways to do the work of justice by seeking God in concentrated times of prayer. Consider devoting a portion of every morning to praying for various needs in your community and around the world. You may also decide to use some helpful resources to assist you and others in the work of prayer, like these:[257]

- The **International Justice Mission** has several resources available including a prayer guide for the abolition of slavery that includes some facts on the two most common forms of slavery—forced labor and forced prostitution. You can access these through their website: www.ijm.org/resources.

- **Pure Hope** is a ministry that seeks to equip churches to pursue sexual purity and oppose sexual exploitation. They provide a variety of resources including prayer guides through their website: www.purehope.net.

- **Exodus Cry** is a prayer movement to end slavery. Download resources from their website and sign up for prayer updates at: www.exoduscry.org.

- The **A21 Prayer Guide** is an informational guide to help you pray for the victims of human trafficking, for the traffickers, for governments, against root causes, for increased global awareness, for the church, and for the A21 Campaign: http://www.thea21campaign.org.

- The Salvation Army has created a resource called **Prayer Guide for the Victims of Sex Trafficking** that includes prayer requests, Scripture passages to prepare your heart and mind for prayer, and much more information about sex trafficking including: Defining the Problem, Scope of the Problem, Demand, and Impact: http://salvationarmyusa.org.

- The **She Is Priceless Devotional** is a five-day devotional designed to lead you through identifying with and praying for victims of sex trafficking. Each day includes a Scenario, how to Imagine yourself in the scenario, Suggested Reading, a Statistic to think on that day, Scriptures to study, and a Prayer Focus: www.sheispriceless.com.

- **One Life Matters** is committed to Jesus Christ and His global mission; using time, money, energy, skills, education, career, advocacy, and every resource to share Christ and serve those in spiritual and physical need. OneLife gives missions a name, a face, and a place. Their Praying for the Exploited Prayer Guide can be accessed at: www. onelifematters.org.

You might also consider planning periodic times during the day for focused prayer. Consider doing a retreat, which will involve praying for the needs of the oppressed. Form a group that will study a particular issue related to justice, and spend considerable time praying with this group.

Finally, study the Scriptures. Fill your mind daily with the truth of God's Word. I recommend a consistent plan of reading, and a plan for memorizing Scripture. Have your own walk through Hyde Park reciting the Scriptures. Mingle prayer with your Scripture reading and memorizing.

But remember Micah tells us to "walk humbly with our God." God-centered humility and Christlike sacrifice stems from one who is walking with God daily through prayer and biblical meditation. Wilberforce was that kind of person. That's the kind of person God uses to do everyday justice.

Wilberforce was a good example, but ultimately, Jesus was the perfect example of living by God's Word, for the good of others, and the glory of God. He humbled Himself, endured the cross, and put the love and justice of God on display. Love the Savior that Wilberforce loved, and love your neighbor like Wilberforce did. Remember that Almighty God loves to use normal men and women, even tiny men like Wilberforce. You are a great candidate for such usefulness.

Conclusion
Longing for a Just World

If you give much thought to the problems of this age very long—grinding poverty, unimaginable slavery, millions of orphans, spiritual emptiness, streets filled with blood, racism, oppression, abuse, abandonment, cancer, AIDS, abortion, tsunamis, illiteracy, pollution, human misery, corrupt governments, death, and more—you'll find yourself longing for a better world.

In your longing for justice, realize that you're really longing for Jesus. For when Christ returns, we'll have perfect justice. We'll experience total shalom, total wholeness. We'll have what our justice-thirsty hearts have always craved.

And we should long for this coming world. And in longing for it, we find hope and power to do justice in this present world. In his classic book *Mere Christianity*, C. S. Lewis says:

> If you read history you will find that the Christians who
> did most for the present world were precisely those
> who thought most of the next. The Apostles themselves,
> who set on foot the conversion of the Roman Empire,
> the great men who built up the Middle Ages, the English
> Evangelicals who abolished Slave Trade, all left their mark
> on Earth, precisely because their minds were occupied
> with Heaven. It is since Christians have largely ceased

> to think of the other world that they have become so
> ineffective in this.[258]

By grasping that the new heaven and earth is in our future, we find sustaining power to deal with the grief of our age and as we get in the middle of the mess that sin has produced. But if you don't have this hope, then this life is as best as it will ever be for you. But you can have more.

This life is not glory. But it's coming. And it's coming for all who place their faith in the Meditator, Jesus Christ, who in His first coming, lived a perfectly just life for unrighteous people, and died a substitute death to make the unrighteous righteous. For those who repent and believe in Christ, they have this assurance: this present life is as bad as it's ever going to be, for in His second coming, suffering will give way to glory. The believer, then, labors and loves with this victorious, eternal perspective. So two questions: (1) Are you laboring for the good of others in this broken world? (2) Are you laboring in hope?

The prophet Isaiah offers four "Servant Songs," which are fulfilled in Christ—who is the ultimate Servant of the Lord. In the first song (Isa. 42), Isaiah mentions "justice" three times in order to describe what the coming Servant will bring. Isaiah describes how Jesus, coming down from heaven, will reorder civilization in the way it was meant to be. God's kingdom *will* come, and God's will, *will* be done on earth as it is in heaven.[259] Isaiah says:

> Behold my servant, whom I uphold,
> > my chosen, in whom my soul delights;
> I have put my Spirit upon him;
> > *he will bring forth justice to the nations.*
> He will not cry aloud or lift up his voice,
> > or make it heard in the street;
> a bruised reed he will not break,
> > and a faintly burning wick he will not quench;
> > *he will faithfully bring forth justice.*

He will not grow faint or be discouraged
    till he has established justice in the earth;
    and the coastlands wait for his law.[260]

Unlike the rulers of Isaiah's day, like Cyrus, the prophet tells us that Jesus won't crush the oppressed; He won't break the bruised reed. Instead, in gentleness, He will defend the weak. The only hope for a truly just world is found in this Messiah. He will show us how beautiful life can be, and will be, and has accomplished this hope for us by paying for it with His own blood.

Until we live in this perfectly just world, let's bring a taste of the future into the present by practicing everyday justice. As we seek to practice kingdom hospitality, care for the fatherless, speak up for the voiceless, love our neighbors, and do justice in other God-glorifying ways, we can do so with songs like this one:

    Truly He taught us to love one another;
    His law is love and His gospel is peace.
    Chains shall He break for the slave is our brother;
    And in His name all oppression shall cease.
    Sweet hymns of joy in grateful chorus raise we,
    Let all within us praise His holy name.
    Christ is the Lord! O praise His Name forever,
    His power and glory evermore proclaim.
    His power and glory evermore proclaim.[261]

Appendix
Recommended Websites

- Children's Hopechest—www.hopechest.org
- Russell D. Moore—www.russellmoore.com
- Christian Alliance for Orphans—www.christianalliancefororphans.org
- Orphan Sunday—www.orphansunday.org
- Desiring God—www.desiringgod.com
- God's Heart for the Orphan—www.saddleback.com/aboutsaddleback/signatureministries/orphancare
- International Justice Mission—www.ijm.org
- World Orphans—www.worldorphans.org
- Journey 117—www.journey117.org
- Hope House International—www.hopehouseinternational.org
- Lifesong for Orphans—www.lifesongfororphans.org
- Adoption Discovery—www.adoptiondiscovery.org
- Abba Fund—www.abbafund.org
- Bethany Children's Services—www.bethany.org
- Reach Orphans with Hope—www.reachorphanswithhope.org
- 147MillionOrphans—www.147millionorphans.com
- Pure Hope—www.purehope.net
- Exodus Cry—www.exoduscry.org
- A21 Prayer Guide—www.thea21campaign.org

- Prayer Guide for the Victims of Sex Trafficking—http://salvationarmyusa.org
- She Is Priceless Devotional—www.sheispriceless.com
- One Life Matters—www.onelifematters.org
- Help One Now—www.helponenow.org
- 127 Worldwide—http://127worldwide.org
- Together for Adoption—www.togetherforadoption.org
- World Relief—http://worldrelief.org
- World Vision—www.worldvision.org
- Free the Slaves—www.freetheslaves.net
- Love 146—www.love146.org
- Polaris Project—www.polarisproject.org
- Not for Sale—www.notforsalecampaign.org
- Hagar International—http://hagarinternational.org/usa

Notes

1. Aristides, "The Apology of Aristides the Philosopher." Translated from the Syriac Version by D. M. Kay. Available online from http://www.earlychristianwritings.com/text/aristides-kay.html, accessed Nov. 17, 2009.

2. Psalm 99:4 ESV, my emphasis. Unless otherwise noted, all Scripture references are from the ESV.

3. Psalm 103:6.

4. See Exodus 22:21–22; Deuteronomy 10:18; 14:28–29; 24:17–22; Zechariah 7:10; Psalm 146:9.

5. See Psalm 68:5, NIV.

6. See Acts 20:35; Galatians 2:10.

7. James 1:27.

8. Matthew 23:23.

9. Isaiah 1:16–17.

10. John Stott, "Foreword" in Gary A. Haugen's *Good News About Injustice* (Downers Grove, IL: InterVarsity Press, 2009), 10, my emphasis.

11. Gary Haugen, "Foreword" in Jim Martin's *The Just Church* (Carol Stream, IL: Tyndale, 2012), x.

12. Stott, "Foreword," in *Good News About Injustice*, 10.

13. My emphasis. No one can seem to locate this popular quote. Several variants of it exist. Whether or not he said it makes no difference to the truthfulness of the statement. It continues to be quoted because it has a ring of truth to it.

14. Martin Luther King Jr. This quote appears several places online, like "Martin Luther King Jr. Day of Service," at http://mlkday.gov/plan/library/communications/quotes.php, accessed Dec. 4, 2013.

15. R. G. Lee, "Payday Someday," available online at http://www.sbc.net/aboutus/sbvoices/rgleepayday.asp, accessed Sept. 6, 2013.

16. "Grace's Story," available online at http://www.ijm.org/node/1499, accessed Oct. 16, 2013.

17. Quotes by G. Von Rad, J. M. P. Smith, and L. Braodt, in Kenneth L. Barker's *Micah*, The New American Commentary (Nashville: B&H, 1998), 113.

18. McComiskey, quoted by Barker, *Micah*, 115.

19. See Exodus 34:6.

20. Tim Keller, *Generous Justice* (New York: Dutton, 2010), 3.

21. Ibid., 3–15.

22. John MacArthur, *Twelve Ordinary Men* (Nashville: Thomas Nelson, 2006), xii.

23. Ibid., 23.

24. Steve Timmis and Tim Chester, *Total Church* (Carol Stream, IL: Crossway, 2008), 63.

25. Job 29:14.

26. John Hartley, *The Book of Job*, The New International Commentary (Grand Rapids: Eerdmans, 1988), 391.

27. Psalm 112:5, my emphasis.

28. Psalm 106:3, my emphasis.

29. Job 29:12–17.

30. Job 31:16–22.

31. Job 31:32.

32. Job 31:1. See also Job 31:9–12.

33. Ephesians 5:7–12, my emphasis.

34. Keller, *Generous Justice*, 93.

35. Ephesians 4:15.

36. 1 John 3:16, my emphasis.

37. Romans 5:8.

38. 1 John 3:16.

39. 1 John 3:18, HCSB.

40. Galatians 6:10.

41. Matthew 5:43–48; 22:37–40; 25:40, 45.

42. Luke 10:37.

43. Luke 10:25, HCSB.

44. Ecclesiastes 3:11.

45. Luke 18:18–30.

46. Luke 10:26.

47. Matthew 22:34–40.

48. Luke 10:29.

49. See Ephesians 2:4–10; Romans 3:21–26.

50. Luke 10:17.

51. Luke 10:20.

52. Luke 10:21.

53. Luke 10:22.

54. Luke 9:51.

55. Luke 18:11.

56. Luke 18:13.

57. Luke 18:14.

58. I heard Daniel Akin use this language in a sermon.

59. Keller, *Generous Justice*, 77.

60. Martin Luther, *Commentary on Romans*, trans. by J. Theodore Mueller (Grand Rapids: Kregal, 1954), xvii.

61. James 2:20.

62. James 2:18–20.

63. James 2:21–26.

64. See Ephesians 2:8–10.

65. Charles Spurgeon, "Serve the Lord with Gladness," sermon online at http://www.ccel.org/ccel/spurgeon/sermons13.xlii.html, accessed Dec. 4, 2013.

66. Timothy Keller, *Ministries of Mercy*, 2nd ed. (Phillipsburg: P&R, 1997), 45.

67. I'm indebted to D. A. Carson for some of these exegetical insights, particularly this point.

68. 1 Peter 2:24.

69. Charles Spurgeon, "The Saddest of the Sad," sermon available online at http://www.spurgeon.org/sermons/2026.htm, accessed Dec. 4, 2013.

70. John Stott, *Issues Facing Christians Today*, 4th edition (Grand Rapids: Zondervan, 2006), 24.

71. Russell Moore, "Letters from a Jericho Ditch: God, Neighbor, and the Questions We Ask," available online at http://www.sbts.edu/resources/magazines/letters-from-a-jericho-ditch-god-neighbor-and-the-questions-we-ask; accessed Nov. 1, 2013.

72. Acts 20:35.

73. Keller, *Generous Justice*, 57.

74. Ibid., xii.

75. Proverbs 3:27.

76. 2 Corinthians 5:14.

77. 2 Corinthians 5:14–15.

78. 2 Corinthians 5:15.

79. 2 Corinthians 8:9.

80. Charles Schmidt, *The Social Results of Early Christianity*, trans. by Mrs. Thorpe, EBook online at http://books.google.com/books?id=X-UROGF6ZcUC&printsec=frontcover&dq=Charles+Schmidt,+The+Social+Results+of+Early+Christianity&hl=en&sa=X&ei=foufUoGtKcbLkQfEtYEo&ved=0CDEQ6AEwAA#v=onepage&q=Charles%20Schmidt%2C%20The%20Social%20Results%20of%20Early%20Christianity&f=false, accessed Dec. 4, 2013, page 328.

81. Luke 6:36.

82. Isaiah 25:6, 8.

83. See Luke 14:12–24.

84. Genesis 3:21.

85. Keller, *Ministries of Mercy*, 41.

86. Ibid.

87. Exodus 29:5.

88. Exodus 33:3.

89. Luke 7:34.

90. See Romans 15:7; 16:5.

91. Galatians 2:11–14.

92. See 1 Corinthians 11:17–34.

93. See Romans 12:13; 1 Peter 4:9.

94. Leviticus 19:33–34, my emphasis.

95. See Genesis 47.

96. Job 31:32.

97. See also James 2:25.

98. Ruth 2:14.

99. Nehemiah 5:14–19.

100. 2 Samuel 9:8.

101. 2 Samuel 9:11, 13.

102. Matthew 10:40.

103. 1 Timothy 3:2; Titus 1:8.

104. Hebrews 13:2.

105. See James 2:1–26.

106. Tim Keller, *Center Church* (Grand Rapids: Zondervan, 2012), 278.

107. Mark 2:13–17; Luke 15:1–2.

108. Mark 9:37.

109. Luke 14:12–14.

110. Matthew 25:35.

111. John 21.

112. Luke 24:13–34.

113. John 14:3.

114. Luke 22:18.

115. Ephesians 2:12.

116. Ephesians 2:13, my emphasis.

117. Robert Karris, *Eating Your Way through Luke's Gospel* (Collegeville, MN: Liturgical Press, 2006).

118. Quoted in *A Meal with Jesus* by Tim Chester (Wheaton: Crossway, 2011), Kindle edition.

119. Mark 10:45.

120. Luke 19:10.

121. Luke 7:34, my emphasis.

122. Chester, *A Meal with Jesus*, Kindle edition.

123. Luke 14:11.

124. Luke 14:12–14.

125. Isaiah 58:6–7, my emphasis.

126. Acts 2:42.

127. John 13:34–35.

128. Keller, *Generous Justice*, 46.

129. Luke 14:14.

130. Ibid.

131. Luke 6:27–36.

132. Luke 6:36.

133. Paul Zahl, *Grace in Practice* (Grand Rapids: Eerdmans, 2007), Kindle edition.

134. Chester and Timmis, *Total Church*, 63, my emphasis.

135. 1 Thessalonians 2:8.

136. Matthew 11:19.

137. I heard my friend Steve Timmis use this phrase at a lecture, along with the point about "our home is not our refuge."

138. You may consider Safe Families for Children network. Safe Families is intended to help at-risk children, and to help their parents get the necessary resources they need in order to maintain custody of their children. Host families can help parents who need to temporarily place their child in a home, due to unmanageable and harsh circumstances. Your family may be able to provide a temporary residence for a child, which typically lasts about six weeks. Unlike foster care, this placement is temporary, you receive no compensation, and the parents voluntarily place their children into selected homes. For more information, see Safe Families for Children and Bethany Christian Services.

139. "International Friendship Program." See http://www.iss.purdue.edu/Programs/IFP, accessed Dec. 2, 2013.

140. Matthew 25:35–36, 40.

141. See Genesis 1:1–2; John 1:1; Colossians 1:16.

142. See John 1:3; Acts 4:24; 14:15; 17:24; Colossians 1:16; Revelation 4:11.

143. See Revelation 10:6; Nehemiah 9:6; Colossians 1:16.

144. See Psalm 8:5–8.

145. Genesis 1:26–27.

146. See Genesis 1:4, 10, 12, 18, 21, 25, 31; 2:18–25.

147. John 17:3. For more on the theological and practical foundations for orphan care, see Tony Merida and Rick Morton, *Orphanology* (Birmingham: New Hope, 2011).

148. See Genesis 2:7, 21–23; 1:27.

149. See Psalm 8; Psalm 104.

150. See Romans 8:18–30.

151. Proverbs 22:2.

152. Proverbs 29:13.

153. Proverbs 17:5.

154. James 3:8–9.

155. Keller, *Generous Justice*, 85, my emphasis.

156. See Richard Wayne Wills Sr., *Martin Luther King Jr. and the Image of God* (New York: Oxford University Press, 2009).

157. Sermon, 1965, Ebenezer Baptist Church. Quote found in Keller, *Generous Justice*, 86–87, my emphasis. He called out the church for not living out this belief, and for not worshipping together. At the National Cathedral, during his last sermon before he was assassinated, he said, "We must face the sad fact that at 11 o'clock on Sunday morning when we stand to sing 'In Christ there is no East or West,' we stand in the most segregated hour of America."

158. Richard Lischer, *The Preacher King* (New York: Oxford University Press 1995), Kindle edition.

159. C. S. Lewis, *The Weight of Glory and Other Addresses* (New York: HarperCollins, 2001), 46.

160. In verse 21, Job seems to say that he hasn't harmed an orphan ("raised my hand") even though he knew the officials would have backed him ("help at the gate") if he wanted to do so. The raised-hand gesture may indicate the way one voted.

161. This is a prayer of lament in the context of an Israelite suffering from vicious attacks, who is crying out for vengeance. I simply note it to point out how the psalmist assumes that being an orphan is awful. For more on this psalm and simply cries for vengeance in Psalms in general, see Derek Kidner, *Psalms 1–72* and *Psalms 73–150*. Tyndale Old Testament Commentary (Downers Grove: InterVarsity Press, 1973), 25–50; 388–91.

162. See 2 Corinthians 8:13–15.

163. Keller, *Generous Justice*, 23.

164. Luke 7:16, my emphasis.

165. Mark 12:38–40; Luke 20:45–47.

166. Keller, *Generous Justice*, 44.

167. 1 Timothy 5:1–16.

168. Aristides, "The Apology of Aristides the Philosopher."

169. James 1:27.

170. See James 1:22–25.

171. See Genesis 21:1; 50:24; Exodus 3:16; 4:31; Luke 1:68; Acts 7:23.

172. Douglas Moo, *The Letter of James* in The Pillar New Testament Commentary (Grand Rapids: Eerdmans, 2000), 97.

173. J. I. Packer, *Knowing God* (Downers Grove: InterVarsity, 1973), 207.

174. In fact, Paul speaks of it in the context of suffering in Romans 8, providing hope and assurance.

175. Galatians 4:6.

176. Ephesians 1:5.

177. Ephesians 5:1.

178. I owe many of these practical ideas to my friend Rick Morton. I highly recommend his book *Know More Orphans* (Birmingham: New Hope Publishers, 2014).

179. Edmund, DeMarche, "Florida Church Flooded with Calls After 15-Year-Old Orphan Asks for Family to Adopt Him." Available online at http://www.foxnews.com/us/2013/10/17/orphaned-florida-teen-makes-adoption-appeal-at-church, accessed Oct. 17, 2013.

180. Louise Boyle, "Orphan Davion Goes to Church." Available online at http://www.dailymail.co.uk/news/article-2463498/Orphan-Davion-Only-goes-church-asks-adopt-him.html, accessed Oct. 18, 2013.

181. My friend Chris Marlow makes this point often. I highly recommend his nonprofit organization Help One Now at www.helponenow.org.

182. Naomi Schaefer Riley, "And the Kids Suffer," *New York Post*. Available online at http://www.nypost.com/p/news/opinion/opedcolumnists/and_the_kids_suffer_97b4wWHF4R2zoOHhCKpSgO, accessed Dec. 4, 2013.

183. David M. Herszenhorn and Erik Eckholm, "Putin Signs Bill That Bars U.S. Adoptions, Upending Families," *New York Times*. Available online at http://www.nytimes.com/2012/12/28/world/europe/putin-to-sign-ban-on-us-adoptions-of-russian-children.html?pagewanted=all&_r=0, accessed Dec. 4, 2013.

184. Kirit Radia, "Putin's Adoption Ban Is Agony for American 'Mom,'" ABC News. Available online at http://abcnews.go.com/International/putins-adoption-ban-makes-american-mom-cry/story?id=18082631#.UONgyI6mG5c, accessed Dec. 4, 2013.

185. Herszenhorn and Eckholm, "Putin Signs Bill."

186. These points were brought home at a recent presentation by Kory Kaeb with Lifesong for Orphans. Visit their website for more information at www.lifesongfororphans.org.

187. Rick Morton makes these points in *Orphanology*, 144–47.

188. Haugen, *Good News About Injustice*, 23.

189. Ibid.

190. Isaiah 1:17, my emphasis.

191. Proverbs 31:8–9.

192. Duane Garrett, *Proverbs, Ecclesiastes, Song of Songs*, New American Commentary (Nashville: B&H, 1993), 246.

193. Ruth 2:22.

194. Ruth 2:9.

195. Daniel Block, *Judges, Ruth*, New American Commentary (Nashville: B&H, 1999), 660.

196. Exodus 1:14.

197. Exodus 4:23; 9:1.

198. Exodus 1:8–22; 3:1–10.

199. Exodus 2:23-25, my emphasis.

200. Christopher J. H. Wright, *The Mission of God* (Downers Grove: InterVarsity Press, 2006), 275–76.

201. I've noted these points in my commentary on Exodus. See Tony Merida, *Christ-Centered Exposition: Exalting Christ in Exodus* (Nashville: B&H, 2014).

202. See Isaiah 19:20–22.

203. See Merida, *Christ-Centered Exposition: Exalting Jesus in Exodus.*

204. Exodus 4:11–12.

204. See Exodus 1.

206. See www.opensecrets.org.

207. C. S. Lewis, *The Screwtape Letters* (Harper Collins e-books), Kindle edition.

208. Pseudonym used to protect identity.

209. Barbara Smith, *From Ashes to Glory: The Pathway to Healing from Sexual Abuse* (Mustang: Tate, 2007), 48.

210. See Psalm 140:12.

211. Smith, *From Ashes to Glory*, 53.

212. See article online at http://www.cnn.com/2010/WORLD/africa/05/19/ghana.school.child.slavery, accessed Dec. 2, 2013.

213. Psalm 68:5, my emphasis.

214. Check out www.purehope.net and www.ijm.org for some Bible study resources.

215. IJM, *The Advocates Handbook: A Blueprint for Building Your Advocacy Campaign*, 20.

216. See Song of Solomon 8:8–9.

217. Smith, *From Ashes to Glory*, 71.

218. See 1 John 2:1.

219. Colin G. Kruse, *The Letters of John*, The Pillar New Testament Commentary (Grand Rapids Eerdmans, 2000), 73.

220. Eric Metaxas, *Seven Men and the Secret to Their Greatness* (Nashville: Thomas Nelson, 2013), Kindle edition.

221. Eric Metaxas, *Amazing Grace: William Wilberforce and the Heroic Campaign to End Slavery* (New York: HarperCollins e-books, 2007), Kindle edition.

222. Metaxas, *Seven Men and the Secret to Their Greatness*, Kindle edition.

223. Ibid.

224. Ibid.

225. Metaxas, *Amazing Grace*, Kindle edition.

226. Metaxas, *Seven Men and the Secret to Their Greatness*, Kindle edition.

227. Ibid.

228. Genesis 3:16.

229. Metaxas, *Seven Men and the Secret to Their Greatness*, Kindle edition.

230. Ibid.

231. Ibid.

232. Ibid.

233. Ibid.

234. Chuck Colson, "Foreword" in William Wilberforce, *A Practical View of Christianity* (Peabody: Hendrickson, eBook edition, 2011), Kindle edition.

235. John Piper, *Amazing Grace in the Life of William Wilberforce* (Wheaton: Crossway, 2006), Kindle edition.

236. 2 Corinthians 5:17.

237. See Habakkuk 2:14.

238. Piper, *Amazing Grace in the Life of William Wilberforce*, Kindle edition.

239. William Wilberforce, *A Practical View of Christianity* (Peabody: Hendrickson, eBook edition, 2011), Kindle edition.

240. In Piper, *Amazing Grace in the Life of William Wilberforce*, Introduction, endnote 7, Kindle edition.

241. Philippians 1:21.

242. Metaxas, *Seven Men and the Secret to Their Greatness*, Kindle edition.

243. Ibid.

244. Ibid.

245. Ibid.

246. Piper, *Amazing Grace in the Life of William Wilberforce*, Kindle edition, my emphasis.

247. Jonathan Aitken, "Foreword" in John Piper, *Amazing Grace in the Life of William Wilberforce*, Kindle edition, my emphasis.

248. See Psalm 115:8; 2 Corinthians 3:18.

249. Spurgeon, "The Lord's Famous Titles," sermon available online at http://www.spurgeongems.org/vols40-42/chs2347, accessed on Sept. 9, 2013.

250. Keller, *Generous Justice*, 6.

251. Bethany H. Hoang, *Deepening the Soul for Justice* (Downers Grove: InterVarsity Press, 2012), Kindle edition.

252. Chris Wright, "I Never Knew Such a God Existed," *Themelios*, Jan. 1992.

253. Colossians 4:12, NIV, my emphasis.

254. See Mark 1:35; Luke 5:16; 6:12; 9:18.

255. Hoang, *Deepening the Soul for Justice*, Kindle edition.

256. Acts 4:29.

257. I'm indebted to my praying wife, Kimberly, for pointing me to these resources. She's an inspiring example of praying for the nations—for gospel advancement and the doing of justice.

258. C. S. Lewis, *Mere Christianity* (Harper Collins e-books), Kindle edition.

259. Ray Ortland Jr., *Isaiah*, Preaching the Word (Wheaton: Crossway, 2005), 273.

260. Isaiah 42:1–4, my emphasis.

261. Lyrics of "O Holy Night," public domain.

INSPIRE OTHERS INTO A LIFE OF MISSION AND JUSTICE WITH THE ORDINARY BIBLE STUDY.

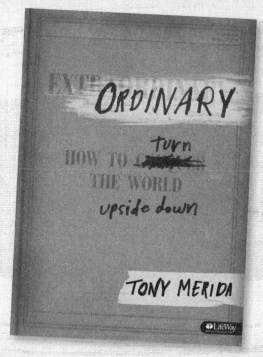

WANT TO SHARE THE ORDINARY MESSAGE WITH YOUR SMALL GROUP?

The *Ordinary* Bible study makes it easy. Each of the six sessions features a 15-minute video from Tony Merida along with *Member Book* exercises to reinforce the teaching. The *Leader Kit* also contains content for group leaders to share on social media, including short video clips from Tony.